A PARENT'S GUIDE TO

ALLERGIES AND ASTHMA

The Children's Hospital of Philadelphia Series

A PARENT'S GUIDE TO ALLERGIES AND ASTHMA

A PARENT'S GUIDE TO ATTENTION DEFICIT
DISORDERS

A PARENT'S GUIDE TO EATING DISORDERS
AND OBESITY

THE CHILDREN'S HOSPITAL OF PHILADELPHIA

A PARENT'S GUIDE TO

ALLERGIES AND ASTHMA

MARION STEINMANN

Foreword by
C. EVERETT KOOP, M.D.

Delta

A Delta Book
Published by
Dell Publishing
a division of
Bantam Doubleday Dell Publishing Group, Inc.
666 Fifth Avenue
New York, New York 10103

Library of Congress Cataloging in Publication Data

Steinmann, Marion.
    A parent's guide to allergies and asthma / the Children's Hospital of Philadelphia ; foreword by C. Everett Koop ; [written by] Marion Steinmann.
        p.   cm.
    Includes bibliographical references and index.
    ISBN 0-385-30029-8 : $10.00
    1. Allergy in children—Popular works. 2. Asthma in children—Popular works.   I. Children's Hospital of Philadelphia.
    II. Title.
RJ386.S74   1992
618.92'97—dc20   91-38747   CIP

Manufactured in the United States of America
Published simultaneously in Canada

May 1992

10 9 8 7 6 5 4 3 2 1

CONTENTS

The Children's Hospital of Philadelphia
Foreword

Several years after I arrived at The Children's Hospital of Philadelphia in the late 1940s, the hospital developed a program for allergic children under the direction of the late Harold I. Lecks, M.D. Allergies, which are caused by an inherited malfunction of the immune system, had become recognizable enough to warrant a special service for children.

Today, we know that allergic disorders are among the most common of all diseases, affecting almost 20 percent of all Americans. For many people, allergies can be occasional nuisances. On the other hand, they can interfere with a child's schooling and can be life-threatening at times.

Dr. Lecks led a collaborative effort within the hospital that resulted in safer, more effective therapy for each child. Working with such disciplines as anesthesiology, pharmacology, psychiatry and rehabilitative medicine, the allergy service made major strides in the management of respiratory failure in childhood asthma and created prototypes for the treatment of these children.

A clinical asthma scoring system, which is now used extensively in pediatrics, was the outcome of the combined efforts of the allergy and anesthesiology sections at the hospital. Under Dr. Lecks's direction, the allergy program had ties with the hospital's affiliates; namely, the Philadelphia Child Guidance Clinic and the Children's Seashore House. It is this strong base upon which the present Children's Hospital of Philadelphia Allergy and Asthma Division is built.

This book takes readers through the causes of allergies to their treatment. It discusses the psychological aspects of allergies and asthma as well as what parents can do to help. It traces these disorders from infancy, the time when a baby may first suffer an allergic reaction to food. The book covers eczema, rhinitis and allergic responses to various drugs and to the venom of certain insects that sting. Asthma is also addressed and there are warnings about some of the controversial unproven procedures that parents may encounter.

The book is pragmatic in terms of offering help to parents and a list of health organizations that provide support.

C. Everett Koop, M.D.
Surgeon-in-Chief Emeritus
The Children's Hospital of Philadelphia

Acknowledgments

This book draws on the expertise and experience of the physicians and other medical personnel at The Children's Hospital of Philadelphia. Founded in 1855, Children's Hospital is the oldest hospital in the country devoted to the care of children. Today, it is a voluntary, nonprofit, 294-bed hospital that is a teaching resource for the University of Pennsylvania School of Medicine. Although the hospital is autonomous administratively, medically and financially, hospital physicians are faculty members of the university. Children's Hospital is affiliated with the Philadelphia Child Guidance Clinic, a separate mental health facility located in the hospital.

Children's Hospital treats children from birth through the age of nineteen, providing primary medical care for many children from its own West Philadelphia neighborhood and highly technical, tertiary care for children from much of eastern Pennsylvania and southern New Jersey—indeed, from all over the world. For over forty years, the hospital has had a group of physicians who specialize in diagnosing and treating children's allergies; the late Harold I. Lecks, M.D., pioneered the hospital's Allergy Clinic in 1949.

The physicians and other medical personnel at The Children's Hospital of Philadelphia and the Philadelphia Child Guidance Clinic who collaborated on this book are the following:

Elizabeth Bailey, CPNP
Clinical Nurse Practitioner
Allergy Division
The Children's Hospital of Philadelphia

Jack Becker, M.D.
Fellow
Allergy/Immunology
The Children's Hospital of Philadelphia

Roger Danziger, M.D.
Fellow
Allergy/Immunology
The Children's Hospital of Philadelphia

John R. Forehand, M.D.
Assistant Physician
Allergy/Immunology
The Children's Hospital of Philadelphia
Assistant Professor of Pediatrics
University of Pennsylvania School of Medicine

Michael M. Grunstein, M.D., Chief
Division of Pulmonary Medicine/Allergy
The Children's Hospital of Philadelphia
Professor of Pediatrics
University of Pennsylvania School of Medicine

James A. Holian, Technician
Pulmonary Function Laboratory

Eva Jakabovics, M.D.
Fellow
Allergy/Immunology
The Children's Hospital of Philadelphia

Lillian P. Kravis, M.D., Senior Physician
Division of Pulmonary Medicine/Allergy
The Children's Hospital of Philadelphia
Clinical Professor of Pediatrics
University of Pennsylvania School of Medicine

Madelaine Nathanson, Ph.D.
Liaison to Asthma Clinic
The Children's Hospital of Philadelphia
Senior Faculty-The Family Training Center
Philadelphia Child Guidance Clinic

Nicholas A. Pawlowski, M.D.
Associate Attending Physician
Director-Allergy Section
Division of Pulmonary Medicine/Allergy
The Children's Hospital of Philadelphia
Assistant Professor of Pediatrics
University of Pennsylvania School of Medicine

Shea Rosen, R.N., Staff Nurse
Allergy Clinic
The Children's Hospital of Philadelphia

Steven M. Selbst, M.D., Director
Emergency Department
The Children's Hospital of Philadelphia
Associate Professor of Pediatrics
University of Pennsylvania School of Medicine

Alberto C. Serrano, M.D., Medical Director
Philadelphia Child Guidance Clinic
Psychiatrist-in-Chief and Director-Psychiatry Division
The Children's Hospital of Philadelphia
Professor of Psychiatry and Pediatrics
Director, Division of Child and Adolescent Psychiatry
Department of Psychiatry
University of Pennsylvania School of Medicine

Sharon K. Sweinberg, M.D.
Assistant Physician
Division of Pulmonary Medicine/Allergy
The Children's Hospital of Philadelphia
Clinical Assistant Professor of Pediatrics
University of Pennsylvania School of Medicine

Ann Zimmerman, R.N.
Day Medicine Unit
The Children's Hospital of Philadelphia

We would also like to acknowledge Shirley Bonnem, Vice President; Dorothy Barnes, her secretary, and the staff of the Medical Library at Children's Hospital.

We would also like to thank the many children and parents and other grown-ups who so graciously took the time to tell us their stories and to share their experiences with allergies and asthma with the readers of this book. To protect their privacy, we have changed their names as well as all other identifying details.

CHAPTER 1

What Are Allergies?

If your child suffers from an allergy, it could be due to a food that he eats, to some substance that he touches, to the venom in an insect's sting, to a medication that he is taking or —so commonly—to invisible particles floating in the air that he breathes.

And your child's allergic symptoms may show up on his skin, in his nose or his eyes, in the airways of his lungs or in his gastrointestinal tract—or in all of these sites and others as well.

- Whenever six-year-old Bobby, for instance, inadvertently eats a peanut or peanut butter or anything else containing peanuts—to which he is highly allergic—he coughs and vomits immediately, and his face itches and swells up.

- Melanie's allergies, on the other hand, show up just on her skin, inside her elbows and on the backs of her knees. From time to time, she gets angry red rashes there, which itch intensely.

- One day recently when five-year-old Geoffrey was taking a sulfa antibiotic, an allergic reaction to the drug caused him suddenly to burst out in hives—some of them the size of silver dollars—all over his body.

• Once when Marjorie was stung by a yellow jacket, as she was dozing in her backyard on a summer day, her allergy to the insect's venom made her left hand puff up alarmingly, to several times its usual size.

• Patricia's allergy is to ragweed pollen. Starting in mid-August every year and continuing until the first frost, the ragweed-pollen season, she suffers from hay fever. Her nose runs profusely and sometimes she sneezes repeatedly. Her eyes and the inside of her mouth frequently itch, and her eyes also often water.

• Jonathan discovered that he is allergic to cats when he stayed overnight with a school friend who has one. Jonathan began having so much trouble breathing that he had to be rushed off to the emergency room of a local hospital for medical treatment. The physicians there explained to his parents that he was having an attack of the lung disease asthma.

Bobby, Melanie, Geoffrey, Marjorie, Patricia and Jonathan are all hypersensitive to substances—such as peanut butter, ragweed pollen and cat fur—that are totally harmless to most people. Such allergies are among the most common of human afflictions. They affect some 17 percent of the population of the United States, according to the National Institute of Allergy and Infectious Diseases, more than 35 million Americans.

Allergies can develop at any time during a person's life, but they most commonly begin in childhood. The symptoms can range widely in severity, as we shall see throughout this book. For many children, fortunately, they are no more than occasional nuisances. However, allergic reactions can trigger attacks of asthma, as in the case of Jonathan, and asthma can sometimes be a very serious, even life-threatening disease. And allergies to foods, drugs and insect venoms can also occasionally threaten a person's life.

Like so many other diseases, allergies tend to run in families. A child who has one parent with allergies has a 50 percent chance of developing some sort of allergy during his or her lifetime. If *both* you and your spouse have allergies, however, each of your children has about a 65 percent chance of developing an allergy. Researchers have not as yet discovered exactly *how* a child inherits an allergic tendency: it seems to be due to at least several different genetic defects. However, they have, in recent years, learned a great deal about what happens inside an allergic child's—or grown-up's—body to produce allergic symptoms.

What Causes Allergies?

If your child has allergies, doctors now know that his symptoms are caused by a malfunction, an overreaction of his immune system, in which it mistakes innocuous substances—such as peanuts or pollen—for dangerous, foreign invaders and mounts an assault on them.

How Our Immune System Works Normally Our immune system is an extraordinarily complicated system whose job is to defend our bodies against bacteria, viruses and other enemies. Our immune system includes many *organs,* dispersed throughout our body: our bone marrow, thymus, spleen, our tonsils and adenoids and our lymph nodes.

These organs produce and provide a home base for *white blood cells*—macrophages, neutrophils, basophils, eosinophils, T cells and B cells—that are the front-line troops that actually fight off invaders. White cells circulate in our blood, constantly patrolling every tissue and crevice in our bodies. Our immune system is continually making new white cells and can finely regulate both their relative numbers and the routes they follow.

As artillery, so to speak, these white-cell troops themselves also make and release a broad array of *molecules,* biochemical substances. The most familiar of these molecules are our *antibodies,* which also circulate in our blood. One particular type of antibody, as we shall see, has a key role in allergic reactions.

Any foreign substance that can provoke these cells and molecules into action is called an *antigen.*

To repel invaders, these organs, cells and molecules work together in many intricate ways. When antigens—one of the many different flu viruses, let's say—enter our body, the macrophages are among the first troops on the scene. These are very large cells (the word macrophage means "big eater"), and they immediately start gobbling up virus particles. So-called helper T cells multiply and send out chemical signals that call into action a second type of T cell—killer T cells. These hunt down and destroy the cells of our body that the virus has infected. Helper T cells also activate our B cells, which, in turn, start making and spewing out vast quantities of antibodies. The antibodies physically latch onto virus particles and help destroy them.

Our B cells reside mainly in our spleen, lymph nodes and the lining of our respiratory and gastrointestinal tracts. The "swollen glands" we sometimes develop in the neck when we are sick are lymph nodes swollen because they are a site of battle against the infection: the lymph nodes are both producing and housing greater numbers of these white-cell troops as well as their artillery.

The next time that we encounter the same strain of flu virus, our immune system "remembers" that it has seen it before and we are therefore immune to it. The first encounter left us with significantly more T cells and B cells able to recognize the virus. We are therefore able to attack the virus more rapidly and with greater strength than the first time around—and we do not get sick from this particular strain of flu virus the second time.

Killer T cells are also constantly patrolling our body tissues for malignant cells: cancer cells continually arise in our bodies, and killer T cells are continually hunting them down and destroying them. Less helpfully, killer T cells also zero in on foreign tissues—such as those in a transplanted kidney or heart—and try to reject them from our body.

What Goes Wrong in Allergies Our immune system can malfunction in many different ways. It can fail to do its job of repelling invaders, thus making a person more susceptible to infections. In acquired immunodeficiency syndrome (AIDS), for instance, the AIDS virus knocks out one particular kind of white cell—helper T cells—with devastating consequences. There are also many inherited immunodeficiency diseases, in which genetic mistakes cause defects in one or more of the immune system's many components. In still another type of malfunction, the immune system can turn against the body itself, producing so-called autoimmune diseases such as rheumatoid arthritis, systemic lupus erythematosus, multiple sclerosis, myasthenia gravis and Graves' disease (the thyroid disorder that affected both President George Bush and his wife Barbara).

In the case of the allergic diseases, what happens is that a person's B cells make—quite unnecessarily—excessively large quantities of one type of antibody.

Our B cells make five major types of antibodies, which doctors also call *immunoglobulins,* each type slightly different in its chemical structure and in the job that it does. Immunologists arbitrarily call these five immunoglobulins gamma, alpha, mu, delta and epsilon, abbreviating them IgG, IgA, IgM, IgD and IgE. IgG antibodies are the familiar "gammaglobulin" that doctors inject to immunize us temporarily against some diseases. The type of antibody responsible for allergic reactions is *immunoglobulin E (IgE).* The normal job of IgE antibodies is combating certain kinds of parasitic infections.

If your child has hay fever due to an allergy to ragweed pollen, it is because he has, in his nose, large quantities of IgE antibodies that his B cells have made specifically against the pollen. These anti-ragweed-pollen antibodies coat the surfaces of certain immune-system cells—called *mast cells*—in the lining of his nose. A lesser amount of these IgE antibodies also coat his basophils (a type of white cell circulating in the blood in very small numbers) and certain other inflammatory, immune-system cells. It is the mast cells, however, that are the main players in allergic reactions.

IgE antibodies work like locks: their molecules contain locklike cavities specifically shaped to receive antigen molecules, which are shaped like keys. Your child's anti-ragweed-pollen IgE antibodies, for example, have "locks" shaped specifically to catch ragweed-pollen "keys." Our immune system generates "locks" in millions and millions of different shapes. We have locks to fit just about any shape of "key" that may happen to come along.

When an allergic child inhales ragweed pollen, ragweed-pollen "keys" combine—within minutes—with his IgE-antibody "locks" on the mast cells in his nose. This causes the mast cells to burst and release powerful biochemical substances called *mediators*.

We have about two dozen of these mediators that researchers have been able to identify so far. The best known is *histamine*. Among the others are leukotrienes, prostaglandins, a substance that activates platelets in the blood, and still other substances that attract eosinophils and other white-cell troops to the site of an allergic reaction.

Allergists do not yet fully understand all the complex actions of these mediators, but together they cause a cascade of biochemical reactions that produce the many diverse symptoms of allergies. In the nose, the mediators cause blood vessels to dilate and leak fluids and tissues to itch and swell and become inflamed. They also cause the mucous membrane lining the nose to produce more mucus.

Once such an allergic reaction starts in a person's nose, there are feedback mechanisms that greatly amplify his symptoms. The mediators attract more and more inflammatory, immune-system cells to the nose. These disrupt its protective lining and allow more and more pollen to penetrate the nasal tissues. This results in the production of even more IgE antibodies, the presence of even more inflammatory cells—and even more itching, sneezing and runny discharge.

Physicians use the term *allergen* for any antigen that can provoke such allergic reactions. They also use the word *atopy* for the tendency for a person's immune system to make excessive amounts of IgE antibodies. Thus the word *atopic* is often used as a synonym for the word *allergic.*

A person never suffers such an allergic reaction the *first* time he or she encounters a given allergen. It takes repeated exposures to ragweed pollen, for instance, over a significant period of time, for an atopic person's immune system to make enough anti-ragweed antibodies to cause hay-fever symptoms.

What a child inherits from his parents, however, is just an *atopic tendency,* a tendency to develop allergies. Precisely what he becomes allergic to is determined both by genetics and by the particular allergens that he happens to encounter in his environment. A child allergic to ragweed does not necessarily also become allergic to other pollens. And it would be quite possible for identical twins—who by definition have identical genes—to develop allergies to different things.

Further, "children's allergic symptoms often show a progression from one organ system to another as the child grows older," notes allergist Lillian P. Kravis, M.D., of The Children's Hospital of Philadelphia. "Usually in infancy it is food allergy or eczema [a skin allergy]. These disorders may later disappear, and respiratory allergies—allergic rhinitis or asthma—may appear. There are exceptions to this sequence, of course, and eczema and asthma may exist together, as may other combinations."

As an allergic person grows older, past middle age, the ability of his or her immune system to make IgE antibodies and mount allergic reactions tends to slack off. Unfortunately, you can't count on it. There are plenty of people around who continue to keep their allergies well into their old age.

The allergists and other physicians at The Children's Hospital of Philadelphia (which is affiliated with the University of Pennsylvania) have had long experience in diagnosing and treating children with allergies and asthma. The hospital's Allergy Clinic was founded more than forty years ago, in 1949.

During the decades since, scientists have vastly increased our knowledge about allergies and what causes them. It was only in the mid-1960s, for instance, that immunologists discovered the existence of IgE antibodies. And in just the last ten years, physicians have developed new methods of diagnosing allergies and asthma and also new medications, and new forms of existing medications, for treating them. Today, modern medications and other measures can control the symptoms of allergies and asthma in the overwhelming majority of children as well as adults. However, as we shall describe throughout this book, many of the most important measures to help children with allergies and asthma are ones that parents can, and must, take themselves at home.

This whole field of immunology and allergy continues to be one of the most rapidly advancing frontiers of medicine. By the time your own children have grown up and become parents themselves, researchers will have devised even more effective treatments for the many children with allergic disorders.

CHAPTER 2

Food Allergies

If your child has a tendency to allergies, a food allergy is one of the types of allergy that can show up the earliest in his or her life. Food allergies can develop within the first few months—or even the first few weeks—of a baby's life.

No one knows how common food allergies really are. They affect, the estimates range, from 0.3 to 7.5 percent of all infants and children. Fortunately, many children who have food allergies when they are babies tend to outgrow them as they grow older (see pages 34–35).

THE SYMPTOMS OF FOOD ALLERGY

If your child does develop an allergy to a food, his symptoms may affect various parts of his body.

Whenever six-year-old Bobby—whom we met in Chapter 1, page 7 and who is highly allergic to peanuts—accidentally eats a potato chip fried in peanut oil, his reaction is immediate. "He usually starts with a lot of coughing," says his mother. "He vomits. His eyes become bloodshot. He itches on his head, his upper arms, around his neck. He is constantly rubbing his eyes. The next thing you know, he starts to swell up under his eyes. Then he starts getting real puffy, little by little, around the cheeks." Once Bobby's eyes swelled up so much that "you couldn't distinguish the bridge of his nose. His face gets so puffy that you can't recognize him. And he starts having trouble breathing."

When five-year-old Stephanie inadvertently eats even a sliver of walnut or any other nut, she too vomits and she also turns red, collapses and becomes lethargic and wheezes when she breathes, says her mother. Once she turned so red "from head to toe that she looked like a burn victim. It took her a good twenty-four, forty-eight hours to get over that."

For one older girl who is allergic to lentils as well as other legumes, the first sign of an attack is often that "my throat starts to get itchy, and sometimes I get hives, mostly on my arms, legs and chest."

One woman vividly recalls her symptoms when she first discovered that she was allergic to shellfish. She was eating crabmeat at a restaurant at the New Jersey shore, and "my fingers and hands started to itch. My eyes and hands started to swell up. I started to wheeze and I was fighting for air. I just wasn't getting enough. I was staggering with anoxia [lack of oxygen] and slurring my speech. I was convinced that I was dying."

These dramatic symptoms—coughing, vomiting, itching, hives, swelling, redness, difficulty in breathing—are all part of the very serious, sometimes explosive, body-wide allergic reaction that physicians call "anaphylaxis." "Ana-" means excessive, and "-phylaxis" comes from a Greek word for protection; this reaction certainly is "excessive protection" against such usually innocuous substances as peanuts, walnuts, legumes and crabmeat.

Anaphylaxis is not unique to food allergies. It can also be caused by allergies to the venoms of some insects that sting (see Chapter 5, page 85) and to certain drugs (see Chapter 6, page 90).

An anaphylactic reaction can start within seconds of a person's eating a food to which he or she is sensitive; it usually starts no later than within an hour or two. The symptoms can also include gastrointestinal pain, cramps, bloating, gas and diarrhea, and in severe cases, it can threaten a person's life.

One dangerous symptom that can develop, allergist Lillian P. Kravis, M.D., of The Children's Hospital of Philadelphia, explains, "is that the tissues of the upper airway around a person's larynx can swell so much that they cut off the air supply." The person may turn blue and become unconscious. The blood pressure may drop. The heart may speed up or beat irregularly, and the person may go into shock, as the cardiovascular and respiratory systems collapse.

A child who has a food allergy may show any of these symptoms of anaphylaxis, alone or in any combination, or he or she may react with much less dramatic symptoms. Food allergies are also linked to the skin condition called eczema (see Chapter 3, pages 37–47). Sometimes a food allergy just causes symptoms similar to those of hay fever (see Chapter 4); whenever two-year-old Margaret eats anything containing wheat, for instance, she begins sneezing, her nose starts running and her eyes get red and watery. Or a food allergy may trigger attacks of the lung disease asthma (see Chapter 7).

It is very rare, however, for a food allergy to produce symptoms that involve only the nose or only the lungs. And most of the time, food allergy symptoms are *not* life-threatening. The most common symptoms—by far—involve only the skin: itching, hives and swelling or eczema.

Whether or not food allergies can also produce symptoms other than these skin, gastrointestinal, respiratory and cardiovascular reactions is a matter of controversy. Recent studies suggest that food allergies may also, in some people, induce migraine headaches. Some parents, however, report that their children experience a variety of other vague or subjective symptoms—nervousness, problems in concentrating, depression, fatigue, restlessness, hyperactivity, muscle aches and pains, bed-wetting—when they eat certain foods. As of this writing, however, no researchers have demonstrated conclusively, with controlled studies, that these other symptoms are indeed due to food allergies.

The danger in your attributing your child's symptoms to a food allergy if allergy is not the real cause is that these symptoms may be signs of some other disease for which your child needs treatment.

THE FOODS COMMONLY PRODUCING ALLERGIES

There is a surprisingly short list of foods that are responsible for most food allergies in both children and grown-ups:

Milk
Eggs
Soy protein
Wheat
Fish
Shellfish
Nuts
Peanuts

Peanuts, despite their name and appearance, are not really true nuts; they do not grow on trees but instead are members of the legume family, relatives of peas, beans, lentils and the like. Stephanie, who is so highly allergic to walnuts and other tree nuts, is not bothered at all by peanuts. "It's really weird," her mother notes. "She can eat peanut butter with no trouble."

There is a much longer list, however, of other foods to which both children and adults can and have developed allergies from time to time. These include:

Oats
Rye
Barley

Buckwheat
Rice
Chicken
Turkey
Beef
Cottonseeds
Sunflower seeds
Sesame seeds
Beets
Corn
Potatoes
Tomatoes
Celery
Spinach
Chick-peas
Apples
Bananas
Oranges
Cantaloupes
Grapes
Mangoes
Pears
Watermelon
Chamomile tea
Chocolate

Usually when a child (or an adult) has a food allergy, he or she is allergic to just one, single food. However, Stephanie is allergic not only to nuts but also to cow's milk and eggs as well as sesame seeds. "That's not common at all," points out Dr. Kravis.

Some children are allergic to many foods in a group, while others are allergic to just one. A study in Denver of fourteen people who were sensitive to nuts found that one person was allergic to five different kinds of nuts, another person was allergic to two kinds of nuts, while the other twelve people were each allergic to just one type of nut.

Curiously, some people have allergic reactions to particular foods only when they exercise strenuously after eating them. One Colorado man, a long-distance runner, would have an anaphylactic reaction whenever he ran after eating shrimp or oysters. Two people—a man and a woman—would have symptoms only if they exercised after eating celery, while one woman reacted only if she played tennis *before* eating celery.

WHAT CAUSES FOOD ALLERGIES?

Whatever particular food your child may be allergic to, the basic physiological reaction in his body causing his allergic symptoms is the same. The reason Bobby, Stephanie and the others are hypersensitive to ordinarily innocuous foods is that their immune systems—as described in Chapter 1, pages 9–14—have mistaken these foods for harmful, foreign substances invading the body, overreacted and made large amounts of IgE antibodies against them. Bobby has IgE antibodies against peanuts in his body, and Stephanie has IgE antibodies against walnuts as well as against cow's milk, eggs and sesame seeds.

If Stephanie accidentally eats even a sliver of walnut, allergenic molecules in the walnut combine with her anti-walnut IgE antibodies, which are on mast cells in her skin and gastrointestinal and respiratory tracts. This causes the mast cells to burst, releasing histamine and the other biochemical substances, the mediators, that produce her allergic symptoms.

You will recall from Chapter 1, page 13 that when a child has an allergic tendency, the specific substances he becomes allergic to depend on what he encounters in his environment. The reason babies develop allergies to foods—as opposed to some other kind of allergen—is that foods are the foreign substances to which they get the most exposure. "For the first three years of life," notes allergist Sharon K. Sweinberg, M.D., of The Children's Hospital of Philadelphia, "there aren't many things that children become allergic to except foods."

And again, the specific food or foods a child develops IgE antibodies against depends on what he or she eats. This is why cow's milk is one of the foods to which babies most frequently develop allergic reactions. "Since milk is almost their sole source of nutrition," says Dr. Kravis, "they are more likely to develop antibodies to it." And Americans, who are so fond of peanut butter, are more likely to develop peanut allergies than people in other countries. Scandinavians tend to develop allergies to fish, and the Japanese, allergies to soy protein and rice.

Infants do not usually have an allergic reaction the first time that they encounter a new food. "Remember, one never reacts to the first dose," Dr. Kravis points out, "but babies can get food antigens through breast milk from their mothers. So although an infant may never have eaten an egg, for example, he could have been sensitized by egg antigens that came through his mother's breast milk."

In some foods, researchers have identified specific allergenic molecules—like all antigens, usually proteins—that cause an allergic person to develop IgE antibodies. In eggs, allergic children usually develop antibodies against two proteins in the egg white, ovalbumin and ovomucoid. In cow's milk, the biggest offender is a protein called beta-lactoglobulin, which occurs in the whey, the watery part of milk, and makes up less than 20 percent of milk protein. Another allergenic protein in cow's milk is casein, the major protein in the curd, the solid portion of milk.

The allergists at The Children's Hospital of Philadelphia recently talked with one mother who did not understand that it is just the proteins in milk that are allergenic. The mother told them that whole milk made her four-year-old son's asthma worse, while milk with only 2 percent milk fat gave him no trouble. "Fat has nothing to do with it," Dr. Kravis points out.

Different children who are allergic to the same food may be making antibodies against different proteins in that food. In a recent study in Detroit of twenty-nine people who were allergic to watermelon, the researchers found that no single protein was allergenic for every one of the twenty-nine.

Sometimes surprisingly tiny amounts of a food can set off an allergic reaction. Barbara, who is allergic to shellfish, was mystified one time when she suffered a severe anaphylactic reaction while she was eating steak at a restaurant. "I was eating steak," she emphasizes, *"not* seafood!" Then the friend who had been sitting next to her at the table told her that she had briefly borrowed Barbara's steak knife to cut her own soft-shelled crab.

However, it is unusual that Bobby is so allergic to peanuts that he reacts to potato chips fried in peanut oil. "Most oils are so purified that people with peanut allergies can tolerate them," explains Dr. Sweinberg, "and someone allergic to corn usually can tolerate corn oil." However, "purification processes vary," adds Nicholas A. Pawlowski, M.D., Director of the Allergy Section at The Children's Hospital of Philadelphia, "and sometimes small amounts of antigens may be retained. People who are exquisitely sensitive may then react to these scant amounts."

You may notice, if your child has a food allergy, that he or she may have a severe reaction to the food on one occasion but not on another. "The severity of the reaction can be affected by a combination of a child's innate allergic reactivity, whether it is mild or severe, and also the amount of the food he or she ingests," explains Dr. Pawlowski. The severity can also be affected by whether a child eats the food alone or with other foods; this affects how rapidly the food is absorbed into his bloodstream from his gastrointestinal tract.

DIAGNOSING FOOD ALLERGIES

There are many reasons other than an allergy why your child may have an adverse reaction after eating a given food. The food may be poisonous or tainted with some toxic substance or contaminated with bacteria or other microorganisms. Or your child may not be able to tolerate a particular preservative or other additive. Some children lack enzymes necessary for digesting certain foods: for example, some are missing the intestinal enzyme lactase, which helps digest lactose, the main sugar in milk. Other children cannot eat gluten, a protein in wheat, rye, barley and oats; doctors call this condition gluten-sensitive enteropathy or, sometimes, celiac disease. Some infants are born with congenital malformations of the gastrointestinal tract that interfere with their digestion. The parasitic disease giardiasis and cystic fibrosis (one of the most common hereditary diseases) can both also cause symptoms mimicking those of a food allergy. And while vomiting and diarrhea can be symptoms of a food allergy, they are more frequently simply due to infections.

If you think your child may have a food allergy, you probably will first want to discuss his symptoms with your pediatrician, who may refer you to an allergist. When you see the allergist, he or she is likely to ask you to describe your child's symptoms very carefully and also what particular food or foods, if any, you associate with these symptoms and how long after eating the food your child's symptoms usually develop. Allergic reactions to food usually occur within an hour or two.

Then, to distinguish a true food allergy from other adverse reactions, your allergist may perform one or more of the following diagnostic tests.

Skin Tests The primary diagnostic test that allergists use to diagnose food allergies is the skin test. In this procedure, the nurse or doctor places a drop of a prepared extract of each food in question on your child's skin.

If your child is allergic to milk, for instance, allergenic molecules in the milk extract will react with antibodies in his or her skin and cause a visible redness and swelling at the spot where the milk extract was placed.

Allergists also use skin tests for diagnosing many other kinds of allergies. See Chapter 8, pages 125–28, for more details on how allergists perform skin tests, what the skin reactions look like and the possible side effects of skin testing.

If you do not already have a list of suspect foods for skin testing, your physicians may ask you to keep a *food diary* for a week or two, writing down every individual food your child eats (including snacks), the quantity of food, the time of day he eats it plus any symptoms that he may experience and also the time that they occur. Such a diary may reveal a relationship between a specific food and your child's symptoms.

Skin tests, however, are not infallible, and skin tests for foods, Dr. Sweinberg points out, "are not as reliable as those for other types of allergens." Your child can have a positive skin test to, say, shrimp, yet have no symptoms when he or she eats shrimp, and vice versa: he or she can have a negative skin test and still be sensitive to shrimp. Allergists therefore sometimes follow up skin-test results with one or more of the following diagnostic tests that involve subtracting or adding suspect foods to your child's diet.

Elimination Diets   First, the physician will have you put your child on an elimination diet for a week or two; that is, he or she will have you eliminate *all* the suspect foods from your child's diet. "But he can have anything else," explains Dr. Eva Jakabovics of The Children's Hospital of Philadelphia, "anything in his usual diet." If your child's symptoms disappear—or fail to appear—it is evidence that one of the suspect foods was indeed causing them.

Occasionally, if the list of suspect foods is long, the allergists will put a child on a very strict elimination diet. "If the child is a baby," continues Dr. Jakabovics, "usually we give him or her what we call 'elemental formulas,' which are hypoallergenic." If the child is older, the allergists usually put him or her on a diet of just lamb, rice and perhaps beets or carrots and pears or apricots. These are all foods that very rarely cause allergies. "We hardly ever have to go down to a diet so restricted, but if a child has multiple allergies, then we are almost obligated to go down."

Food Challenges   Next, after a week or two of the elimination diet, the allergists will reintroduce the suspect foods— one at a time—and see what happens. Allergists call this a food challenge. They start with a very small amount of the suspect food, "a tiny sample of milk, say," says Dr. Jakabovics, "only a fifth of a teaspoon or so." If your child shows no symptoms, the allergists then have him eat increasingly larger amounts of the suspect food. If at any point your child does have any reaction, they immediately stop the challenge: it is evidence that the suspect food is indeed a culprit —and that your child should avoid eating it.

One morning recently, Dr. Jakabovics performed a food challenge on ten-month-old George, who had been having episodes of wheezing when he breathed and who also had positive skin tests to wheat and several other foods. She handed George a tiny piece of a wheat cracker, less than a quarter of the cracker. George licked at it and chewed on it and before he got around to finishing the piece, within less than twenty minutes, he began—Dr. Jakabovics could hear with her stethoscope—to wheeze. She immediately stopped the food challenge. "At this point we feel that George has a wheat allergy, so now he should not eat any wheat products at all."

Sometimes, when a child's symptoms are very clearly *not* life-threatening—and as mentioned earlier, most of the time, they are not—"we feel comfortable," continues Dr. Jakabovics, "having parents do food challenges at home. It is much cheaper for them and much more convenient." Margaret had only hay-fever-like symptoms and when she was about a year old, her allergist had her mother perform a food challenge at home. First, she put Margaret on an elimination diet for a while, and then "when I added back wheat, it was bad. She got a terrible runny nose. Since then, I have kept her off wheat. And it has worked. She is doing real well."

CONTROLLING FOR PSYCHOLOGICAL FACTORS "There is a considerable emotional component involved with food and with eating," Dr. Pawlowski points out, "and children may create or complain about nebulous 'symptoms' as a way—consciously or unconsciously—of gaining attention or as a way of rebelling, a way of saying 'No!' to their parents. And parents sometimes misconstrue this as symptoms of an allergy."

With a ten-month-old baby like George, however, "the question of an emotional reaction to a food is not that significant," Dr. Jakabovics explains. "George is too young to just look at a food and start wheezing or show other symptoms that may be unrelated to an allergic reaction." Therefore, George's—and also Margaret's—food challenges were what allergists call *"open" challenges:* the children, as well as their parents, could see what foods the children were eating.

With an older child, however, the allergists control for psychological factors by concealing the suspect foods in capsules. The child and parents—as well as the doctor or nurse observing the child's reactions—are "blind"; that is, they do not know which foods are in which capsules. Doctors call this type of procedure a *"double-blind" food challenge.*

The allergists further control for psychological factors by putting a placebo—that is, a nonallergenic substance (usually sugar)—in some of the capsules. Such a *"double-blind placebo-controlled food challenge"* is the most definitive test of whether a person does indeed suffer an adverse reaction to a particular food.

If a child does show any symptoms after swallowing the

placebo-filled capsules, it is evidence that psychological factors are involved. "If he or she reacts to a sugar pill," explains Dr. Jack Becker of The Children's Hospital of Philadelphia, "then we know that the reaction is not due to an allergy."

"However," adds Dr. Pawlowski, "if a child repeatedly shows true allergic symptoms when he or she undergoes double-blind placebo-controlled food challenges, then that secures the diagnosis of a food allergy."

FOOD CHALLENGES IN THE HOSPITAL When a child does have severe, life-threatening reactions to food, the allergists perform food challenges in the hospital, where they can continuously monitor the child's vital functions, such as his heart and respiration rates, with electronic equipment and where the staff can keep him under close observation.

One day recently at The Children's Hospital of Philadelphia, Dr. Becker and Ann Zimmerman, R.N., performed a food challenge on twelve-year-old Florence. Florence's parents have had to rush her to hospital emergency rooms thirteen times for anaphylactic reactions after eating catsup, salad, pork and beans and turkey stuffing—dishes that all contain many different ingredients. The question was: which ingredient in these foods was causing the problem? Both Florence and her mother thought it was the tomatoes.

Dr. Becker and Nurse Zimmerman also inserted an intravenous tube into a vein in Florence's hand so that if she did develop a severe reaction, they could quickly treat her with intravenous drugs or fluids. At twenty-minute intervals, Becker had Florence swallow capsules filled with increasing doses of ground dried tomato—although neither she nor her mother nor Zimmerman (the "blind" observer) knew what was in the capsules. After each round of capsules, Zimmerman took Florence's blood pressure and had her blow into a small device called a peak-flow meter, which measured the rate at which she could expel air from her lungs. The first dose was 250 milligrams (less than 1/100 of an ounce) of tomato; the second, 500 milligrams; then one gram, two grams, four grams, eight grams (in sixteen capsules). By mid-afternoon Florence had swallowed a total of thirty-three capsules containing 15.75 grams of dried tomato, but while she was becoming very skilled at swallowing capsules, she failed to have—the monitors and tests showed—any adverse reaction to the tomato. Dr. Becker then had her eat, in an open challenge, several pieces of a real tomato. She still had no symptoms. Whatever was sending Florence to emergency rooms so often, it was not tomatoes.

The allergists at The Children's Hospital planned to have Florence repeat this procedure, on another day, with capsules filled with dried onion and green pepper.

Laboratory Tests   There are also some laboratory tests that allergists sometimes use to help diagnose food allergies. These can measure the quantity of IgE antibodies in a sample of your child's blood to specific food antigens—that is, anti-peanut or anti-walnut (or anti-any-other-allergenic food) IgE antibodies.

Unorthodox Tests   Parents may occasionally encounter several controversial tests and treatments for food allergies. See Chapter 8, pages 145–48, for a discussion of such unorthodox diagnostic methods and therapies.

"Food allergies, I think, are underdiagnosed," notes Dr. Sweinberg. "A lot of people have the lesser symptoms and don't realize that they are due to a food allergy." Conversely, the allergists at The Children's Hospital of Philadelphia see many parents who believe that their children have food allergies when they do not. "We have people come in here all the time saying, 'I am allergic,' but when we do a food challenge like the one we did on Florence, many times it doesn't come out positive."

TREATING FOOD ALLERGIES

When children do suffer severe allergic reactions to foods, physicians treat them by giving them injections of *epinephrine (adrenaline)* and also usually *antihistamines,* by mouth or sometimes by injection or intravenously. Sometimes doctors also prescribe *corticosteroids,* by mouth, injection or intravenously. These medications are also widely used to treat many other forms of allergies; see Chapter 8, pages 129–30 and 135–41, for more about these drugs, what they accomplish and their possible side effects.

In very serious cases, doctors may also have to give a child supplemental oxygen, pump out his or her stomach to remove any remnants of the offending food and, occasionally, admit him or her to the hospital.

Physicians advise that the parents of a child who has a life-threatening food allergy carry with them, at all times, both antihistamine and epinephrine. There are kits available, about the size and shape of a pen, that contain an easy-to-use syringe already filled with epinephrine. Stephanie's allergist has given her mother a prescription for such a device. Mrs. F. now carries one, plus an antihistamine, all the time and has also given a second one to Stephanie's nursery school, "just in case."

LIVING WITH FOOD ALLERGIES

There are no drugs or shots that can prevent symptoms in children (or grown-ups) who have food allergies. The only way to prevent these reactions is for your child to avoid completely eating the offending food or foods.

This is why it is important for you to have physicians not only diagnose whether or not your child's symptoms are due to a true food allergy, involving IgE antibodies, but also identify the specific food or foods responsible. It makes no sense for you to go to a great deal of trouble having your child avoid a long list of foods, especially common staple foods, if he or she is not truly allergic to them.

The allergists at The Children's Hospital of Philadelphia sometimes meet parents who are unnecessarily withholding a particular food from their child's diet. "Mothers tell us all the time that their children are allergic to milk," says Dr. Kravis, "and that milk causes mucus and nasal congestion. The grandmothers are saying, 'Stop the milk.' We hear this over and over again. Overproduction of mucus secretions all through the respiratory tract is indeed one of the hallmarks of allergy, but only if a child is truly allergic to milk. You have to establish the fact that an allergy is present. The message is, don't remove the milk—or any other staple food—until you have your child tested for allergy."

Constant Vigilance   If diagnostic tests show that your child is indeed allergic to a specific food or foods, you will find that you must exert constant vigilance to keep your child from eating the offending food. "We must monitor everything he eats, everything," emphasizes six-year-old Bobby's mother, "and everywhere he goes, every person he is in contact with, we must tell them right away that he is allergic to peanuts and peanut oil and that he can't eat anything with them in it.

"You just have to let everybody be aware of it—his school, family, friends, all our relatives, all the parents of his friends, everybody.

"And everything we buy, everything that comes into this house," Mrs. J. continues, "we always have to read the labels all the way to the end."

"You have to be so careful," adds five-year-old Stephanie's mother. "I never put anything in her mouth without checking the list of ingredients first, as much as is humanly possible. No one wants to get behind me in the aisles at the supermarket," she laughs. "I scrutinize everything!"

HIDDEN INGREDIENTS You will discover that many allergenic foods can hide in less-than-obvious places.

Wheat is often a thickener in soups, sauces, gravies and salad dressings and a filler in meat loaf and sausages.

Eggs find their way into mayonnaise, custard and hollandaise sauces, some noodles and pastas, soufflés, meringues and marshmallows.

Milk is a constituent of creamed soups and vegetables, cream sauces, mashed potatoes, macaroni and cheese and many breads, cakes and other baked goods.

Peanut oil is a particularly sneaky ingredient: cooks use it precisely because it is tasteless and odorless.

Cottonseed flour can be concealed in cookies, breads, cakes, crackers, doughnuts, baby cereals and candies. One man allergic to cottonseed ate two pieces of candy on his lunch tray on an airplane—and immediately had an anaphylactic reaction.

QUERY RESTAURANTS Conscientious parents also find themselves asking questions in restaurants. "I have even done this at our local fast-food restaurant," says Stephanie's mother. "I've asked to see the list of what's in their products. Surprisingly enough, they were very understanding. They were very nice, and they showed me. It turns out the only thing in there— unless they change things—that Stephanie has to be leery of is the rolls: some of them have sesame seeds on them." Some fast-food restaurants now are posting or have booklets available with information about their ingredients.

When one woman allergic to peanuts wants to eat in a Chinese restaurant, "I always ask ahead if they are using peanut oil. I am also constantly asking about nuts on top of ice cream, because sometimes they use peanuts and sometimes other nuts."

It is a good idea for you to keep on querying restaurants. In these days of creative and eclectic cooking, you never know what imaginative ingredient a chef might decide to add to a classic dish. "Somebody's secret ingredient," notes Dr. Becker, "could be something very different from what you expect."

HAVE YOUR CHILD WEAR A TAG   Physicians suggest that a highly allergic child wear—at all times—a necklace or bracelet with a tag giving information about his or her allergies. Stephanie used to wear a necklace with such a tag, "but I think there is a visibility problem with a necklace," says her mother, "because people don't really see it. It's tucked inside the shirt sometimes." So Stephanie now wears a bracelet telling about her allergies and giving her name, both her pediatrician's and allergist's names and also her family's as well as her doctors' telephone numbers.

FIND ALTERNATE FOODS   If your child is allergic to a major, staple food, you will have to, of course, provide substitute foods. Some children who are allergic to cow's milk can tolerate goat's milk. Others drink one of the soy-protein infant formulas on the market; there are also soy cheeses, soy yogurt and soy-based ice creams. However, the Food and Drug Administration recently warned parents against feeding babies soy-based beverages other than the infant formulas as their sole source of nutrition. Not all "soy drinks" or "soy milks," the FDA emphasizes, are nutritionally complete, but some health food stores, says the FDA, have erroneously told consumers that they are. (Still other children, of course, can be allergic to soy protein.)

With two-year-old Margaret's allergy to wheat, her mother has had to use considerable ingenuity to find alternatives. "For bread, I substitute specialty breads. There is a rice bread and a potato bread and a pure rye bread, although most rye breads do have wheat in them. She eats corn pasta, corn spaghetti. Cereal is easy; there are a lot of cereals that are made just from oats. For cookies, there are oat-based and fruit-based cookies. The wheat-free fig bars are her favorites."

* * *

The allergists at The Children's Hospital of Philadelphia see children and others with life-threatening food allergies who do not take them seriously enough. Food allergies can be life-threatening, as we have emphasized; they do occasionally kill a person. In one widely reported incident, an eighteen-year-old college freshman, who was allergic to peanuts, died of anaphylactic shock after eating two bites of a chili that a restaurant chef had unexpectedly seasoned with peanut butter. Another college student, who was allergic to cottonseeds, died within minutes of eating a cookie that contained them. A sixteen-year-old boy, who was allergic to nuts, died from eating ground pecans in the crust of a cheesecake, and another person, allergic to fish, died after eating french-fried potatoes that a cook had fried in oil previously used to fry fish.

"Trouble comes to those who are careless," emphasizes Dr. Pawlowski, "as are so many teenagers, or those who do not inform themselves about the contents of the foods they eat."

Dr. Jakabovics encountered one such teenager recently. Fifteen-year-old Raymond is so highly allergic to nuts, shellfish and cottonseeds that he should have a syringe of epinephrine with him at all times—but this day he had left it at home. "You should carry it with you," Dr. Jakabovics told him. "That's the purpose. It should be in your pocket all the time. You never know when you might want to eat a cookie or something, and you can get sick from that. You could need the medicine, and it's at home in the medicine cabinet. That's not a good practice."

Nevertheless, parents can do everything right, and still a child can get into trouble. Stephanie suffered a life-threatening attack in nursery school one day—and her mother *had* carefully explained Stephanie's food allergies to the people at the school; Stephanie carried her own snacks to school each day, and she also wore a necklace with a tag telling about her allergies. Despite all these precautions, someone at the school gave Stephanie a piece of birthday cake with walnuts in it. Stephanie had an anaphylactic reaction, and her frightened mother had to rush her off to her pediatrician for emergency treatment.

The problem is that there are an endless number of people a child may encounter who have had no experience with food allergies and have no way of knowing how serious they can be. "I am sure the woman at the school had no idea Stephanie's allergies could be life-threatening," says her mother.

"The misconception is that it is just going to cause you discomfort," notes one woman with significant food allergies. "People think that you are going to have swelling or wheezing or something like that. The majority can't imagine what it's like not to be able to breathe."

WHAT HAPPENS AS A CHILD GROWS

Fortunately, many of the children who develop food allergies when they are infants will tend to grow out of them as their bodies mature. "Most babies," explains Dr. Kravis, "outgrow their allergies to milk and eggs and also sometimes to other foods."

George, at ten months, now must avoid wheat and wheat products, but "in a year or so," explains Dr. Jakabovics, "we will skin test him again and challenge him again with wheat. There is a strong possibility that this child will outgrow his wheat allergy."

Stephanie, at age five, already seems to be losing her allergy to milk. Under her allergist's supervision, her mother has been cautiously rechallenging her, starting with one teaspoon of milk a day. "But she has no taste for it," says Mrs. F. "The kid won't even eat ice cream!"

However, some other children do *not* grow out of their food allergies. "I know a nine-year-old," says Dr. Kravis, "who still goes into shock if he gets even the tiniest bit of milk inadvertently. This is very unusual."

And some foods—among them, nuts, peanuts, buckwheat, shellfish and cottonseed—provoke allergies that are particularly persistent. There are people who are so allergic to these foods that they must spend their entire lives avoiding them.

And children and grown-ups of any age can suddenly become allergic to a food that he or she has been eating all along without any problem. Barbara, for one, was in her mid-thirties when she abruptly discovered—when she had an anaphylactic attack in the midst of a seafood dinner at the New Jersey shore—that she had developed an allergy to shellfish.

CHAPTER 3

Skin Allergies

If your child has any sort of blemish on his or her skin—a rash, red or scaly patches, blisters or swelling—there are innumerable possible causes, ranging from infections to insect infestations to simple irritation. There are three different types of these skin disorders that are due to allergic reactions. Physicians call them *eczema* (or, often, atopic dermatitis), *hives and angioedema* and *contact dermatitis.* In this chapter, we will discuss eczema through page 47, hives and angioedema on pages 47—51 and contact dermatitis on pages 51–58.

ECZEMA (ATOPIC DERMATITIS)

If your child has an allergic tendency, eczema—like a food allergy—is one of the earliest ways it can manifest itself. Eczema may show up in the first few months of a baby's life. "Eczema usually makes its appearance in infancy," notes allergist Lillian P. Kravis, M.D., of The Children's Hospital of Philadelphia. "Approximately 60 percent of cases appear in the first year of life."

Eczema is the most common way that allergies can affect a child's skin. Surveys show that it affects up to about 4 percent of all children. "It is a very big problem," adds Dr. Kravis.

Your doctor is likely also to use the term "atopic dermatitis" for this condition. The word "atopic" means allergic (you recall from Chapter 1, page 13); the word root "derm-" means skin, and "-itis," inflammation. So the term "atopic dermatitis" simply means an allergic inflammation of the skin.

THE SYMPTOMS OF ECZEMA

If your child has eczema, he or she may have a red rash or tiny blisters on his or her skin. The child's skin is often inflamed, very dry and scaling or flaky, and it may also become thickened and coarse. Sometimes it is crusty, with an oozing, weeping discharge.

Five-year-old Johnny's eczema, for instance, started when he was about six months old as a "bad rash around his groin area, on his back, patches just about all over," says his mother. When Johnny and his mother saw Dr. Eva Jakabovics at the Allergy Clinic at The Children's Hospital of Philadelphia recently, his mother reported that his skin was getting worse. He had a bad area on one thigh; he had pinkish lesions an inch or so in diameter on his back, where it looked as if his skin had simply come off, and sometimes, said his mother, "he has a rash all over his arms."

Above all, however, eczema *itches*. Flare-ups usually start with itching, and physicians often say that eczema is not so much a rash that itches as "an itch that rashes." They mean that it is the child's scratching to relieve the intolerable itching that causes most of the damage to his or her skin.

When Johnny "walked into my room," Dr. Jakabovics noticed, "he immediately started scratching himself all over. He doesn't stop scratching for more than two or three minutes at a time." Johnny's mother adds, "In every video and movie we have of our family, there is Johnny scratching. It is constant,

constant. Sometimes you look at his skin and wonder what happened. It looks as if a rake has gone across it, from the scratch marks."

And one mother of a baby girl who has eczema reports, "When I go upstairs to check on her at night, she will be sound asleep and yet she is still scratching, scratching, scratching."

Melanie is old enough to understand that "scratching makes it worse and makes it spread more. But it itches so much, you can't help it. I wake up in the night; I know I shouldn't scratch," she confesses, "but I just can't not do it."

Curiously, eczema tends to occur in particular places on a child's body and "the *location* of eczema depends on the child's age," notes allergist Sharon K. Sweinberg, M.D., of The Children's Hospital of Philadelphia. In babies, the lesions typically start on the face (often the cheeks), the head and neck, and the *outside* of the elbows and knees. In older children, the location usually shifts to the *inside* creases of the elbows and the knees.

Teen-aged Melanie's distribution is classic: on the backs of her knees and inside her elbows. "When it is really bad," she explains, "it spreads all the way down to my wrists, but not up my arm too much, and it is around my neck, up under my ears, sometimes up around my chin and face. And I sometimes get a rash on the backs of my hands and between my fingers."

What can happen as a child continues to scratch is that the lesions may become infected. "We see a lot of children with very severe, infected eczema," says Steven M. Selbst, M.D., Director of the Emergency Department at The Children's Hospital of Philadelphia. "Occasionally—maybe half a dozen times a year—we see children with eczema that is so badly infected we need to admit them to the hospital for treatment. It is sometimes a true emergency."

Eczema can also affect a child's eyes. Ophthalmologists call this "atopic keratoconjunctivitis." "Kerato-" means the cornea of the eye; the "conjunctiva" is the membrane covering the eye, and "-itis," you recall, means inflammation. In rare cases, this condition can be so severe that it permanently damages the eyes and results in the loss of vision.

A child's eczema typically comes and goes for years, flaring up from time to time and then subsiding again, sometimes according to the seasons. Melanie finds that hers is worse in the summer. "It seems as if the heat aggravates it. Whenever it is hot, and I get sweaty or grimy, it makes me feel itchy. In winter, I might be clear of it for a couple of months, and then when spring comes, I get a patch again. In the summer, it is pretty persistent."

More often, children's eczema is better in summer. "The sun seems to help Johnny's skin," says his mother. "His legs will clear up. His chest looks better, but the rash in his groin will stay on. For him, the fall and winter are definitely worse."

What Causes Eczema?

The fundamental cause of a child's eczema is unknown. In many children, however, the disorder is linked to specific allergies.

In about 20 to 30 percent of children with eczema, allergies to foods cause the eczema to flare. "In infancy, when eczema usually makes its appearance," says Dr. Kravis, "it is frequently related to food." When these children eat foods to which they are sensitive—researchers at Johns Hopkins University have shown with double-blind placebo-controlled food challenges (see pages 26–27)—their skin usually starts to itch immediately and a rash may appear several hours later. One breast-fed infant was allergic to eggs; his eczema cleared up completely when his mother removed eggs from her diet. When she did eat an egg again, in a food challenge, his symptoms reappeared within twenty minutes after he nursed.

Like all children with food allergies (see Chapter 2, page 20, and Chapter 1, pages 11–12), these children have developed IgE antibodies against specific allergenic molecules in particular foods. When they eat these foods, these allergens combine with the antibodies, which are on the surfaces of mast cells in their skin. This causes the mast cells to burst and release histamine and the other biochemical substances, the mediators, which in turn cause the symptoms of eczema.

In some children, flare-ups of eczema are linked with allergies to substances that float in the air—such as pollens—that the child may inhale. See Chapter 4, pages 61–66, for a discussion of the many different airborne substances that can cause allergic reactions.

Physicians do not really know whether such allergies to foods or airborne substances are the primary cause of eczema or merely secondary, aggravating factors. "There is a big question," notes Dr. Kravis, "as to whether these allergens actually *cause* eczema or whether they just cause itching of existing eczema, and then the child's scratching makes it worse." Researchers believe children with eczema may well also have some other abnormalities of their immune systems.

One thing that is known is that children with eczema tend to come from atopic families. Two thirds of them have parents or siblings who also have eczema or who have hay fever or asthma. Melanie's mother and sister, for instance, both have hay fever, and her mother's father had asthma.

Studies of twins show that eczema has a strong genetic component. Among identical twins (who by definition have identical genes), if one twin has eczema, the other also has the disorder 85 percent of the time. In the remaining 15 percent of cases, the twins apparently, at some point in their lives, were exposed to some different environmental factor or factors. Fraternal twins (whose genes are different) share eczema no more often than do other siblings.

Of children who have eczema, 50 to 80 percent eventually go on to develop hay fever or asthma. "It is very hard to predict whether this will happen," says Dr. Kravis, "but that's why it's important for a parent to find out whether a skin rash is indeed eczema. Eczema is a manifestation of a constitutional allergic predisposition to overreact." If your child has eczema, "you shouldn't be surprised if he also wheezes when he has a cold or when he exercises, because he has hyperreactive skin and hyperreactive airways in his lungs. That's part of his atopic inheritance."

DIAGNOSING ECZEMA

"Not all skin rashes are eczema, of course," emphasizes Dr. Kravis. There are many other types of skin inflammations that can resemble eczema, as can scabies (which is caused by mites) and also some fungus infections. Eczema can also look very much like allergic contact dermatitis (which we discuss later in this chapter).

Nevertheless, physicians can often diagnose whether or not your child's rash is indeed eczema simply by looking at it. "We can pretty much diagnose eczema by its *appearance,*" says Dr. Sweinberg, and also by its *characteristic distribution* on a child's body. "Its location helps us, as well, and the *itching.* Especially in our atopic children with asthma, a rash is most likely to be eczema."

Skin Tests To find out whether or not specific foods or airborne allergens are involved with your child's eczema, allergists may order *skin tests.* These detect whether there are IgE antibodies in your child's skin against specific foods or inhaled substances. See Chapter 8, pages 125–38, for more information about how doctors perform skin tests, what they show and their possible side effects.

Of children with eczema, 80 percent do have positive skin tests to some food or other substance; this is particularly likely to be the case in children who also have hay fever or asthma. However, 20 percent of children with eczema have negative skin tests, "so you can't always pinpoint the cause," says Dr. Kravis. In Johnny's case, for instance, his skin tests all were negative.

Elimination Diets and Food Challenges If your child's skin tests do point a finger toward a possible food allergy, allergists may follow them up by having you put your child on an *elimination diet* and then subsequently performing—or have you perform at home—*food challenges,* such as we described in Chapter 2, pages 25–28.

TREATING ECZEMA

Avoiding Allergens If your child's physicians are able to demonstrate that an allergy to a given food is causing your child's eczema to flare, then he or she should avoid eating that food. As mentioned in Chapter 2, there are no drugs or shots that can prevent allergic food reactions in susceptible children. See also pages 29–34 of that chapter for a discussion of how you can help your child live with a food allergy.

Similarly, if allergies to any inhaled substances are aggravating your child's eczema, then he or she should avoid these substances, if possible. See Chapter 9, pages 151–58, for tips on how to help your child avoid airborne allergens.

Medications Whether or not your doctors are able to link your child's eczema with allergies to any particular food or airborne substance, there are medications that can help keep his or her eczema under control.

ANTIHISTAMINES One of the most important things to do is to reduce your child's itching, to prevent the damage he does to his skin with his constant scratching. For this, physicians prescribe antihistamines by mouth. Antihistamines work relatively fast; they may reduce the intensity of your child's itching within a half-hour or so.

CORTICOSTEROIDS To clear up your child's skin lesions themselves, doctors prescribe corticosteroids to be applied topically; that is, you spread the medication directly on the patches of eczema. Corticosteroids have an anti-inflammatory action, and they should be used just until the lesions heal. Melanie found that the steroid "was amazing, very effective. It really cleared them up." Occasionally, physicians suggest a steroid-impregnated tape, which comes in a roll like adhesive tape. "You cut off a piece and just cover the bad areas," Dr. Kravis explains. "You put that on until the areas clear, and then you stop using it."

For more information about antihistamines and corticosteroids, which physicians prescribe for many different types of allergies, see Chapter 8, pages 129–30 and pages 137–41.

ANTIBIOTICS If your child's eczema does become infected, physicians prescribe antibiotics, most often by mouth. "We see a lot of parents who neglect a child's eczema," says Dr. Selbst. "They've run out of cream, or they haven't been using the cream on the child's skin, or they haven't taken him to the doctor for the last year. The child continues to scratch, and the eczema gets infected."

Good Skin Care There are also skin-care routines that can help you keep your child's eczema under control, says Dr. Nicholas A. Pawlowski, Director of the Allergy Section at The Children's Hospital of Philadelphia.

KEEP YOUR CHILD'S SKIN MOISTURIZED Children with eczema usually have very dry skin, and this dryness tends to make the itching even worse. Therefore, doctors advise using some sort of moisturizer on a child's skin. "This is just as important as the corticosteroid," Dr. Jakabovics emphasized to Johnny's mother. "And it's not just putting it on. It is pouring it on. You should have your hand full of the cream and then rub it into his skin until it is absolutely absorbed. It might take thirty minutes. He should be so greasy you will be afraid that he will slip out of your hand. A big jar of moisturizer shouldn't last you more than about a week."

"The best time for parents to apply steroid and moisturizing creams," adds Dr. Sweinberg, "is right after your child takes his bath." This is because the moisturizing agents help seal the moisture from the bath into your child's skin.

How often a child with eczema should take a bath is a question about which physicians disagree. Some recommend that parents give the child a bath only every other day. Others recommend daily baths. "How your child takes a bath is also important," says Dr. Pawlowski. "The skin's normal function as a barrier and its natural oils are impaired by baths that are too long and at very high temperatures. An additional common error is to allow your child to play with the soap, so that his skin is exposed to harsh, soapy water for a prolonged period of time."

PREVENT SCRATCHING Doctors also advise parents of children with eczema to keep their fingernails trimmed short to minimize the damage done by scratching. Dr. Kravis noted approvingly to Johnny's mother, "You do have his nails cut short." Sometimes doctors suggest that you cover the eczema to reduce scratching. "Some children do all their scratching at night," says Dr. Kravis, "so that if you cover it at night, they can't get to it. They can't scratch."

AVOID CONTACT WITH IRRITANTS Children with eczema also tend to have skin that is easily irritated by contact with substances that do not bother others. Melanie finds that she cannot wash with the same *soap* her parents use. "It makes my skin feel really tight and dry, almost too squeaky clean. It is a very uncomfortable feeling." Doctors suggest using a mild, neutral soap without any fragrance. "We tried several different soaps," says Melanie, "and we finally discovered a couple that are more soothing to my skin."

Another irritant, sometimes, is the *detergent* that is used in washing the child's clothes. Recently, when Dr. Kravis saw a young fellow with eczema around his groin, she suggested that his mother try a different brand of detergent. "This is an area where there is a lot of perspiration," Dr. Kravis explained, "and it can leach out any residual detergent that wasn't rinsed out in the laundry cycle. And then his underwear fits closely enough there that it can rub against his skin. You might consider having him wear boxer shorts that fit more loosely."

Some children with eczema have skin easily irritated by *wool* or *synthetic fabrics*. "Wool feels sort of prickly," says Melanie. "I don't wear wool because it is so scratchy. I have just one wool sweater that I wear occasionally, a dress sweater." Another girl finds that she can wear wool "if it's a really nice soft wool and I wear a turtleneck underneath."

WHAT HAPPENS AS A CHILD GROWS

"The prognosis for a child with eczema is really good," says Dr. Kravis. As with food allergies, "the chances of growing out of mild eczema, even severe eczema, are very good. Fifty percent of the children will lose it by the age of five, and another twenty-five percent by adolescence. And there is nothing left. You would never know that your child had ever had any skin disease."

Dorothy, for example, who is now in her twenties, suffered from eczema—at times it was conspicuous on both her face and her hands—from the time she was a baby, all throughout elementary school and also junior high school. Then, gradually, she started to outgrow her eczema; the flare-ups became less and less frequent. "Sometime in college," Dorothy reports, "I discovered that my skin wasn't so sensitive anymore." Today, Dorothy has a lovely, clear complexion, with nary a trace to show that her skin was ever any different. "I can't recall the last time I really had eczema," she says. The only remnant is that "when it's really hot and humid, and I get sweaty, I sometimes get a tiny, itchy patch for a day or so."

HIVES AND ANGIOEDEMA

Another way that your child's allergies may show up on his or her skin is in the form of hives. Some 10 to 20 percent of us experience at least one episode of hives at some point in our lives. Your physician is likely to call them "urticaria," a name that comes from the Latin word for nettle. "Urticaria," says Dr. Pawlowski, "is not an uncommon problem among children."

THE SYMPTOMS OF HIVES

Hives have a very different *appearance,* you will notice, from the skin lesions caused by eczema. A single hive looks something like a mosquito bite: it usually has a central, raised area, surrounded by a larger zone of reddened, inflamed skin. Doctors call the raised area, the bump in the middle, a "wheal"; the larger red zone, a "flare"; and the whole thing, a "wheal-and-flare."

Your child can have a single hive or many, and they may appear on virtually any part of his or her body. They may occur as tiny, discrete bumps, or they may coalesce into "giant hives," huge affairs covering much of your child's arm or leg. "There are many gradations of hives, which may take many forms," notes Dr. Kravis. Like eczema, however, hives also *itch* intensely.

Hives are sometimes accompanied by *swelling* of the child's underlying tissues, a condition that physicians call "angioedema." ("Angio-" means pertaining to the blood vessels, and "-edema" means swelling.) "Usually angioedema involves a child's eyes, the ears and the lips," notes Dr. Kravis. "The genital area is also very sensitive to that sort of swelling." While hives occur in the superficial layers of a child's skin, angioedema occurs in deeper layers of the skin where there are few nerve endings. Unlike hives, angioedema does not itch, but it can be painful or burn.

One five-year-old boy's arms and legs once puffed up so much that "I turned into a dragon!" he chortles. "I looked like an alien!" He holds out his hands, curving his fingers into claws, to demonstrate.

Another five-year-old, from time to time, gets hives on his feet. They swell up so much, his mother reports, that he cannot get his shoes on. His brother gets hives on his cheeks, "straight down the side of his face."

Angioedema can be life-threatening if the tissues of the child's airway, around the larynx, swell so much that they cut off his or her supply of air. Hives and angioedema can also signal the body-wide, life-threatening allergic reaction called anaphylaxis. (See Chapter 2, pages 16–17.) "Generalized hives are usually the first sign of anaphylaxis," emphasizes Dr. Kravis. "And then it cascades, affecting the respiratory system, causing low blood pressure and eventually shock.

"So generalized hives is an important manifestation. If it happens once, it isn't a cause for great concern, but if it is a recurrent problem, then it is. One or two discrete hives do not mean so much, but if a child has generalized hives, parents should definitely bring it to the attention of their physician."

WHAT CAUSES HIVES AND ANGIOEDEMA?

If your child breaks out in hives, one possible cause is an *allergy* to a particular *food*. The most common symptoms of food allergies, as we saw in Chapter 2, page 17, are those involving the skin: itching, hives and swelling, or eczema. Whenever six-year-old Bobby—whom we met earlier and who is highly allergic to peanuts—inadvertently eats anything cooked in peanut oil, his head, his neck and his upper arms begin to itch, and his face and eyes swell up so much, his mother says, that he becomes unrecognizable.

Another possible cause of a child's hives and angioedema can be an *allergy to insect venom or to a medication,* as we shall see in Chapter 5, pages 84–85, and in Chapter 6, page 90.

Occasionally, a child will break out in hives from an *allergy to a substance that he inhales.* See Chapter 4, pages 61–67 for a discussion of the many different airborne substances that can cause allergic reactions.

A child may also get hives from simply *touching* something to which he or she is allergic: one fifteen-year-old girl gets them whenever she lets her dog lick her arm.

These allergens—foods, insect venoms, medications and airborne and other substances—all produce hives, angioedema and anaphylaxis by the same mechanism, involving IgE antibodies, that we described in Chapter 1, pages 11–13. This is also the same immune mechanism that helps cause some children's eczema to flare (see pages 40–41). When these allergens bind to IgE antibodies on mast cells in the skin, the cells release histamine and other biochemical substances, the mediators, which produce the allergic symptoms. No one knows why this mechanism aggravates eczema in some children and causes hives and angioedema in others.

Children—and adults—can also develop hives, angioedema and even anaphylaxis from *nonallergic causes,* such as exposure to certain physical stimuli: some people get hives simply from pressure on their skin or from vibrations, or when their skin is chilled or heated, or is in contact with water or is exposed to sunlight. Others get these symptoms after exercise; this is apparently related to a rise in their interior body temperature.

Hives and angioedema can also be a sign of many *other diseases* and conditions, including reactions to blood transfusions, certain rare tumors and viral, bacterial and fungus infections. "Very often," notes Dr. Pawlowski, "a child will have a flare-up of hives in association with a viral upper-respiratory infection."

DIAGNOSING HIVES AND ANGIOEDEMA

Physicians—and many parents—can usually recognize hives and angioedema when they see them, but finding out what is causing them is more difficult. Your doctor is likely to ask you whether your child has eaten any new foods recently or has been stung by an insect or is taking any medications. As with eczema, if doctors suspect a food allergy, they may order *skin tests* (see Chapter 8, pages 125–28) to detect IgE antibodies in the skin against specific foods. If any of these skin tests are positive, the doctors may suggest an *elimination diet* followed by *food challenges* (Chapter 2, pages 24–28) to prove the cause-and-effect relationship between the food allergens and the skin problems. See Chapter 5, pages 88–89, and Chapter 6, pages 92–94, for a discussion of how physicians diagnose hives due to allergies to insect venoms and to medications.

If your child suffers recurrent episodes of angioedema, it is particularly important for you to have your physician try to find out the cause. These attacks can be due to a serious—but rare—hereditary deficiency of a regulatory protein in the blood. "While hereditary angioedema is not an allergy," says Dr. Pawlowski, "it can resemble an allergic kind of problem. We don't see very many of these children, but they can have significant, life-threatening attacks, and they sometimes go undiagnosed." There are specific laboratory blood tests to distinguish this hereditary form of angioedema, and doctors can treat these children with medications.

In many cases, however, hives and angioedema are "what we call idiopathic," says Dr. Sweinberg. "That is, we are unable to determine the cause."

However, emphasizes Dr. Pawlowski, "It is still important

that physicians systematically investigate each child's case, looking for those causes that he or she can avoid."

TREATING HIVES AND ANGIOEDEMA

If your child's hives and angioedema are due to an allergy to a food or other allergenic substance, the best treatment is for him or her not to eat the food or to avoid the offending substance.

Physicians generally prescribe *antihistamines* to reduce the itching. If hives and angioedema are extensive, doctors may inject the child with *epinephrine (adrenaline)*. Sometimes, to quell a severe episode, they prescribe *corticosteroids* by mouth for a short period of time. See Chapter 8, pages 129–30 and 135–41, for more information about these medications, which are widely used to treat many different allergic conditions.

As with children who have life-threatening allergies to foods, parents of children who are subject to massive hives and angioedema should carry with them, at all times, an antihistamine and a kit containing an easy-to-use, already-filled syringe of epinephrine.

Most of the time, however, children's hives are mild and go away without trouble. When one boy gets them on his cheeks occasionally, his mother gives him an antihistamine and puts on a cold compress, and "they are gone in about forty-five minutes."

CONTACT DERMATITIS

Your child can also develop allergic reactions to substances that he or she *touches,* substances that, again, are harmless to most other people. Physicians call this third type of allergic skin disorder "contact dermatitis."

A child's contact dermatitis can look—and itch—very much like eczema: a rash or tiny blisters; inflamed, reddened skin, sometimes dry, sometimes moist and oozing, and if a child scratches his skin, it too can become infected.

DIAGNOSING CONTACT DERMATITIS

If your child has contact dermatitis, physicians can often— as with eczema—diagnose it simply on the basis of its *appearance*. "A contact allergic reaction," Dr. Kravis points out, "is often confined to one area of a child's body." One of the biggest clues to what substance is causing the dermatitis is its exact *location,* precisely where on your child's body it occurs. However, "with contact dermatitis," notes Dr. Sweinberg, "you have to be a little more of a detective than with eczema."

"In infants," Dr. Kravis explains, "contact dermatitis is generally caused by the baby's allergy to the laundry *detergent* that is used for washing his clothes, or to the *fabric softener* or *drier sheets.* Some of those things are notorious for causing contact dermatitis. One infant whom we saw recently had dermatitis around his neck, where his clothing was coming in close contact with his skin, and also on his thighs; he was wearing tights of some kind. We are not certain, but we think that his dermatitis is from the detergent. From its location, that seemed reasonable. Or an infant can get contact dermatitis from whatever *baby oil* or *creams* or *lotions* that his mother is putting on his skin."

In older children, Dr. Kravis continues, "allergies to *fabrics and dyes* can cause a contact reaction, sometimes when children sleep with their dolls or other toys." One little girl, Shirley, developed a rash that "started at her neck and was just all over her body. She was peppered with little red spots," says her mother. "She scratched and cried and was very uncomfortable." It turned out that the rash was due to an all-in-one, pink stretch suit of a synthetic fabric, which covered Shirley from her neck down to her feet and wrists.

"Sometimes," adds Dr. Sweinberg, "you'll see dermatitis on

a child's feet. This can be due to an allergy to *leather* or to *rubber* in shoes. Or to the *dyes* on shoes; that is a very common cause of contact dermatitis in children."

"In teenagers," continues Dr. Kravis, "allergies to *makeup, cosmetics* and *toiletries* are a problem." Soaps, shampoos, after-shave lotions, moisturizing creams, suntan creams and hair sprays, dyes and other hair dressings can all cause contact dermatitis. The allergenic ingredients in these products are often the *perfumes* or *preservatives*. Again, location is the biggest clue to the cause: dermatitis around the mouth points toward an allergy to lipstick or toothpaste; on the scalp and forehead, allergy to some hair preparation, and around the neck and wrists, allergy to a perfume. One girl developed an itchy rash under her arms when she used one brand of deodorant—but she had no trouble with other brands. One adult woman's eyelids became swollen and itched from, she thought, her husband's cigarette smoke—but when her allergist suggested that she try not using eye makeup for a while, her eyelids soon returned to normal.

"Another thing that can cause a lot of problems around the eyes is nail polish," adds Dr. Kravis. "That isn't so obvious. People are always touching their face, but they are not aware of it, and the eyes and eyelids are the most sensitive area of the face."

Children can also develop contact dermatitis because of allergies to various topical *medications,* medicines applied directly on the skin: antihistamines, antibiotics, anesthetics such as benzocaine and, again, often to the preservatives in these medicines. One girl is allergic to something in one brand of adhesive tape; it caused a raised, red welt, precisely the size and shape of the tape, when she used it to cover up a sore on her back. There are also a variety of contact allergies that can affect the eyes, allergies to medications or preservatives in eyedrops or in contact lens solutions.

Dermatitis on both earlobes or around the neck or a wrist or finger can be due to an allergy to *jewelry*—earrings or a necklace, bracelet, watch or ring. The offending substance in jewelry is usually the metal nickel. About 2 percent of teen-aged girls and 10 percent of all adult women, studies show, are allergic to nickel, but only about one out of every hundred men are. And by the time women have reached their fifties, some 15 percent of them have a nickel allergy.

Sometimes to help identify the culprit substance causing a child's contact dermatitis, "if we are greatly perplexed," says Dr. Kravis, the allergists use a type of skin test they call a *patch test:* they apply the suspect substance to cloth or paper and tape it to the skin of the child's upper back or arm for forty-eight hours or so.

Poison Ivy   Perhaps the most familiar example of allergic contact dermatitis in children is poison ivy and its relatives, poison oak and poison sumac. All three plants contain an oily chemical called urushiol; if your child is allergic to one of these plants, he or she probably is allergic to all three. There are also other plants that, less commonly, can cause similar skin reactions. One is a primrose, *Primula obconica,* sometimes called "poison primula."

Like other allergies, sensitivity to urushiol is acquired; a child is never allergic to poison ivy the first time he or she gets into it. Poison ivy allergy is rare in very young children, who have not yet been exposed much to the plant, and is most common in adults. Not everyone, however, does develop the allergy. There are people who can handle these poisonous plants without getting any skin eruptions.

What often happens is that a previously sensitized child brushes against a poison ivy plant and gets a little urushiol on some part of his body. It starts to itch; he scratches it; and before anyone realizes what is happening, he may spread it all over his body.

"Most parents can diagnose poison ivy by themselves," notes Dr. Kravis. The patches tend to be on exposed parts of a child's body: hands, arms, ankles, legs, face. "They are usually streaklike, with a linear distribution," explains Dr. Sweinberg, "usually with small blisters and redness. Oftentimes, it is a moist type of skin lesion." In severe cases, the lesions can coalesce and weep profusely, and become infected.

HOW SUBSTANCES CAUSE CONTACT DERMATITIS

Contact dermatitis is caused by an allergic mechanism different from the one involving IgE antibodies that is responsible for food allergies (see Chapter 2, page 20), flare-ups of eczema in some children (see page 41) and many cases of hives (see page 49).

The contact allergic reaction instead involves the immune-system cells called T cells (see Chapter 1, pages 9–10). If your child is allergic to, say, poison ivy, whenever he gets some urushiol oil on his skin, allergenic molecules in the oil combine with specific urushiol receptors on T cells. This causes the T cells to produce biochemical substances called lymphokines, which cause the skin symptoms. Similarly, a child with a contact allergy to a laundry detergent has T cells with receptors specifically shaped to combine with allergens in the laundry detergent.

In contrast to allergic reactions involving IgE antibodies, which occur quickly—a child allergic to peanuts, you will recall, reacts immediately when he eats them—these contact allergic reactions involving T cells take some time to develop. Poison ivy rashes do not break out immediately when a child touches a plant but typically appear twenty-four to forty-eight hours later. Physicians call this type of allergy a "delayed hypersensitivity."

Your child can also develop rashes that look very much like allergic contact dermatitis but that do not involve his immune system; they are instead due to direct irritation of his skin. Strong acids and some detergents can cause this nonallergic type of contact dermatitis. Patch tests (see page 54) cannot distinguish allergic from nonallergic contact dermatitis, but this does not matter much since the treatment is usually the same.

TREATING CONTACT DERMATITIS

Once you or your physician figure out what probably is causing your child's contact dermatitis—whether it is a detergent, a fabric, a toiletry or a piece of jewelry—"the best thing to do," Dr. Kravis advises, "is simply to remove whatever it is or stop using it and see what happens."

When the doctor told Shirley's mother that the synthetic stretch suit was causing Shirley's all-over rash, "I really didn't quite believe him," Mrs. N. admits. "The doctor said, 'Don't put that suit on Shirley again, and the rash will go away. You don't really have to do anything else.' So I put the little pink suit away and never put it on her again, and indeed the rash did go away."

There are hypoallergenic brands of cosmetics on the market, but, notes Dr. Kravis, "It's amazing how very hard it is to convince people to stop using makeup or to change brands. It's as though you were banishing them to a desert island somewhere."

Sometimes physicians suggest that a child take *antihistamines,* by mouth, to stop the itching of contact dermatitis, and they may also prescribe a *topical corticosteroid* to reduce the skin inflammation. For very severe cases, such as massive poison ivy (or poison oak or poison sumac) they may prescribe a course of *corticosteroids* by mouth. "Once every few years," says Emergency Department Director Dr. Selbst, "we see a child with a case of poison ivy so severe that we have to admit him or her to the hospital." For more about these medications, which are also widely used for many other types of allergies, see Chapter 8, pages 129–30 and pages 137–41.

Preventing Poison Ivy The best way to treat poison ivy is not to get it. You should learn, and also teach your children, what it—and also poison oak and poison sumac—look like. Poison ivy is a shrub or vine that bears slightly glossy leaves in groups of threes and has grayish-white berries. It often grows along the sides of roads and the edges of woods, as well as in suburban backyards; one favorite spot is inside privet hedges. However, poison ivy is very variable in appearance. Children should follow the old rule: "Leaflets three, let it be." One woman, a serious gardener, says, "I never touch *any* plant with clusters of three leaves unless I know it —by name—as something else." All parts of the poison ivy plant are poisonous, and while summer is the most usual time for children to get into poison ivy, the allergenic oil remains in the dead stalks, and can get on a person's skin and clothes even in winter.

Poison sumac grows as a shrub or as a small tree and has compound leaves; that is, it has pairs of leaflets arranged along a stem with a single leaflet at the end. Poison oak, too, grows as a shrub or as a vine, and has leaves that somewhat resemble those of oak trees. It is difficult, however, to learn how to identify these plants from a description, or even pictures, in a book. The best way for you to learn them is to get someone who knows these plants well to point them out to you.

Obviously, if you have any of these plants growing in your own backyard, you should try to get rid of them, particularly if you have a toddler around. There are herbicides that can help eradicate them; these must be used carefully, however, because they can damage other vegetation. You should never burn these plants, because the poisonous oil can be carried in the smoke and "be blown around," Dr. Kravis points out, "and it is still allergenic." Once in the air, the oil can get not only onto a person's skin but also into the eyes, nasal passages, throat and lungs.

If your children are going to be out walking around where these plants may grow, having them wear long-sleeved shirts, long pants and socks can help keep them from getting the oil on their skin. However, the oil can easily get on clothing—or a pet's fur—and persist for a year or more. One girl broke out in a mysterious rash one winter, and no one suspected poison ivy because of the season; it turned out that she was in the habit of toweling off her dog, every day, when he returned from his romp in the woods. Another woman, a city-dweller, was surprised to suffer a bout of poison ivy when she had not been out of the city for weeks. She finally remembered that—weeks earlier—on a visit to the country, she had set her camera down on the ground in the woods; apparently it picked up some poison-ivy oil. You can also get poison ivy from a sweater or other clothing stored away from the season before.

You can help your child prevent poison ivy—or reduce its severity—by washing the oil off his or her skin promptly. One woman, who lives in a suburban area so heavily infested with poison ivy that it's hard to avoid, keeps a bar of strong, yellow laundry soap handy in her kitchen. Whenever she thinks that she may have inadvertently touched or brushed against a poison ivy plant, she scrubs the exposed skin thoroughly as soon as she gets home.

CHAPTER 4

Allergic Rhinitis ("Hay Fever")

Like most people you probably call this disorder "hay fever" or perhaps "rose fever," but these terms are both misnomers. Neither hay nor roses is the most common cause of the disorder nor does it involve a fever. Your doctor is more likely to use the term "allergic rhinitis" for this annoying condition. "Rhin-" means nose, and "-itis" means inflammation, so the word rhinitis simply means an inflammation of the mucous membranes lining the nose.

Allergic rhinitis is the most common of all the allergic diseases; it affects 10 to 15 percent or more of the population of the United States.

THE SYMPTOMS OF ALLERGIC RHINITIS

If your child has allergic rhinitis, whenever he inhales pollen or some other substance floating in the air to which he is sensitive, his nose reacts immediately, usually within a half-hour or so. He may sneeze repeatedly, often violently, convulsively. Angela's record so far—her two brothers have carefully tallied—is seventy-four consecutive sneezes. A child's nose may also drip like a leaky faucet or run profusely with a clear, watery discharge. Thirteen-year-old Derrick, before he was treated, was constantly blowing his nose, "all day long," says his mother, "using boxes and boxes of tissues."

The eyes may become red and also run. Five-year-old Caroline's eyes would water so copiously that they fogged her glasses so much she could not see out through them. The eyes often also itch, as do the nose, the inside of the mouth and the throat.

"It is this itchiness," emphasizes allergist Lillian P. Kravis, M.D., of The Children's Hospital of Philadelphia, "that really distinguishes allergic from nonallergic rhinitis."

With time, a child's nasal passageways may become stuffed up and congested, often to the point where he must breathe through the mouth. One grown-up recalls that when she was a child, her nose was so constantly clogged that one of her nightmares was that robbers would bind and gag her (as she had seen so often in movies and on television) and that she would suffocate because the gag would keep her from gulping in enough air.

When a child must breathe through his mouth like this, "his mouth gets dry, and his throat gets sore," Dr. Kravis continues. "That's a very common complaint. A child complains of a sore throat in the morning a great deal, and it isn't due to an infection."

And nasal secretions dripping down the back of his throat —what physicians call a "postnasal drip"—can also cause a child with allergic rhinitis to cough a lot.

While allergic rhinitis can begin at any age, the symptoms typically start later in a child's life than do allergies to foods or allergic eczema. "It's rare in infants," Dr. Kravis points out. "Babies don't often have hay fever, because they haven't yet had enough exposure to pollens."

Suzanne, for instance, was ten when her parents realized that the "summer cold" she got in the middle of August every year was actually due to an allergy. And Katherine was thirteen when she first recognized she had the symptoms. "I was at summer camp in the Poconos, and I would be standing out in the middle of this field of grass as they raised the flag every morning, with tears streaming down my face—and they weren't from emotion." Most people who are going to develop allergic rhinitis do so before they are out of their teens.

Not infrequently, children will suffer from allergic rhinitis for years before their parents realize what it is. One high school teacher, who is very familiar with the symptoms because she herself has it, notices that "a lot of the kids are not being treated. I don't think their parents recognize what it is. They think that the kids have colds." And children themselves do not always complain; they do not always realize that not everyone's nose itches or drips constantly and that other children can routinely breathe through their noses.

The Common Airborne Allergens

Pollens Of all the multitudes of invisible substances wafting about in the air, the pollens, explains Dr. Kravis, are probably the most common causes of allergic rhinitis.

Pollens are the male reproductive cells of flowering plants. The plants with showy, colorful and fragrant flowers—such as roses—are not responsible for much allergic rhinitis; they tend to have large, heavy, waxy pollens and rely on insects to carry them from one flower to the next. (Florists, gardeners and other people who work with flowers, however, do sometimes become allergic to these pollens.) Instead, it is the plants with drab, inconspicuous flowers that are the big troublemakers. These tend to have fine, light pollens and utilize the wind to disperse them. These plants spew out large quantities of dry, dustlike pollen grains that can ride currents of air for vast distances.

Plants, of course, follow the seasons in flowering and releasing their pollens, and children with pollen allergies therefore sneeze and sniffle according to the calendar. In the Philadelphia area and much of the northeastern United

States, the trees pollinate during the spring, from March through June. Those with allergenic pollens include many of the most common, native species that line our streets and fill our parks and forests: oaks, maples, beeches, ashes, birches, elms, poplars, sycamores, hickories, mulberries, sweet gums, walnuts. From mid-May to mid-July, the grasses are pollinating. Among the common offenders are timothy, fescue, orchard grass and June grass. The weeds (among them plantain and lamb's-quarter) overlap the grasses. They start pollinating in May and continue into the fall. In mid-August, the biggest culprit of all—ragweed—begins letting loose its pollen and continues through October.

Botanists ironically have given ragweed the scientific name *Ambrosia*—the food of the gods. Under the microscope, ragweed pollen even *looks* evil: the spherical grains are covered all over with sharp spines. A single ragweed plant can let loose a million such pollen grains a day, and scientists have collected them four hundred miles out at sea and two miles up in the air.

Farther north, the allergy season is shorter: the trees start pollinating later in the year, and the weeds finish earlier. Farther south, the season is longer, and across much of the Deep South, some sort of pollen is in the air most of the year. In other parts of the country, other species contribute: olive, eucalyptus, pecan, mountain cedar, palm, mesquite, cottonwood, tumbleweed. Allergists in your area have charts showing which pollens are the most prevalent in your part of the country during which months of the year.

In contrast to food allergies—where children most often are sensitive to only one food—with allergic rhinitis "children usually are not allergic to just one pollen," says Dr. Kravis. And different people have symptoms on different schedules. Five-year-old Caroline, who is allergic to several trees and grasses, "every year, starts about the beginning of March," says her mother, "and lasts until, I'd say, the beginning of July." Katherine is also allergic to trees and grasses but her symptoms start later and finish sooner than Caroline's because she is allergic to different species. "I start about the first of May," says Katherine, "sometimes a little earlier. And around Memorial Day, that's my peak." And Suzanne suffers *two* bouts of allergy symptoms each year: she has a spring tree-pollen season, skips the summer grass-pollen season but has a second season starting in mid-August, thanks to ragweed, and lasting until the first frost.

It is these seasonal symptoms due to pollen allergies that laymen (and physicians) often call "hay fever"—whether or not the timing of the symptoms actually coincides with the haying season in their area.

A child's symptoms can vary considerably from year to year, and also from day to day within a pollen season, depending on the vagaries of the weather. Pollen levels are often highest on dry, windy days, but there is much local variation. You should not be surprised if the ups and downs of your child's symptoms bear little relationship to published pollen counts. The counts are often made in a single place, the day before, and may or may not even include the specific pollens to which your child is allergic.

Molds Many substances in the air other than pollens can cause a child to suffer allergic rhinitis the year around. Among these are the molds, which are simple, nearly microscopic plants that thrive in damp places in our houses: basements, crawl spaces, window and door frames, the soil around houseplants, food storage areas, garbage cans, bathrooms (on plumbing fixtures and shower stalls and curtains) and upholstery, and in vaporizers, air conditioners and humidifiers. What gets into the air and what your child can inhale are the spores (the reproductive cells) and bits of the threadlike filaments.

Molds also flourish out-of-doors, during the growing season, in soil and in vegetable matter; their levels peak in the late summer and early autumn and are at a minimum when snow covers the ground. In theory, these outdoor molds can thus produce seasonal symptoms, but in practice, mold seasons are usually less clear-cut than pollen seasons.

Seven-year-old Charlie, however, who lives at the New Jersey seashore where it is very humid, does have a mold season. Charlie starts having "a real rough time by the middle or the end of August," says his mother. "The mold levels are high then, and they are starting to dry off and blow around. We really have to watch him until around Halloween."

"I have trouble with molds if I have a lot of plants around," adds one adult, who lives in a dry, Western state. "And I can tell you if it's going to rain. It may be that as the moisture moves in, it activates all the molds."

House Dust and House-Dust Mites   Another frequent cause of children's year-round sniffles is house dust, which is a complex mix of household debris: remnants of foods; lint from clothing, curtains, carpets and upholstery; pollens and molds; bacteria and other microorganisms; fragments of bodies of dead insects and also their feces; and dander—that is, minute bits of hair and scales of skin—from dogs, cats and other pets as well as from us humans.

The primary villains in house dust, however, allergists have realized since the 1960s, are microscopic, insectlike creatures called *house-dust mites*. These are actually not insects but arachnids, eight-legged relatives of ticks and spiders. These dust mites feed on human dander and therefore thrive in vast numbers in our homes—in carpets, curtains, upholstered furniture, soft toys, clothing and, above all, in our bedrooms, particularly in our mattresses, pillows and other bedding. One gram (0.035 ounce) of house dust can easily contain a thousand individual dust mites. Entomologists have aptly named one of the most common dust mites *"Dermatophagoides."* "Dermato-" comes from the Greek word for skin, and "phagoides" from a word for eat; the long name simply means "skin eaters." Scientists have identified and purified at least five different allergenic proteins in dust-mite bodies and feces. Dust mites grow best in the warm, humid summer months, but a child's symptoms can be worse in the winter when the windows are closed and the heating system may blow mite particles around the house. "The use of a vaporizer or humidifier," adds allergist Sharon K. Sweinberg, M.D., of The Children's Hospital of Philadelphia, "can also increase the numbers of dust mites in winter."

Other allergens that can find their way into household dust include *kapok* (a plant material used to stuff pillows, mattresses and boat cushions) and *feathers*. Researchers have recently come to realize that *cockroaches*—which proliferate so abundantly in so many city apartment buildings—are also extremely allergenic. There are two species, a native American cockroach and an imported German one, and both of them, like the house-dust mite, have allergenic substances both in their bodies and in their feces. Emphasizes Dr. Kravis, "Cockroaches are a big factor in precipitating children's allergic rhinitis."

Animal Danders   Other causes of year-round symptoms are emanations from the pets we keep around as companions and friends. Many, many children are sensitive to *cats*. Charlie is so allergic to them that one day in school when he reached into his buddy's backpack to take out a toy car, within ten minutes his eyes swelled up—because the classmate's cat had been sleeping on the backpack. So far researchers have found that cats make at least seven different allergens. The main one is in their fur and skin and also in their saliva, and there are others in their blood and urine. "A lot of people don't realize that the saliva and the dander are both important," notes Dr. Kravis. And cats, of course, freely spread their saliva around the house as they lick their fur clean and then repeatedly rub against doorways, furniture and the legs of their humans. A recent study at the Mayo Clinic confirms what people with cat allergies have been telling each other for years: that some cats are more allergenic than others. The researchers found that some cats shed one hundred times more allergens than others.

"*Dogs* are probably less allergenic than cats," observes Dr. Sweinberg. As is the situation with cats, there are a number of different allergenic proteins in dog dander, urine and saliva. Charlie's mother discovered that he also has a dog allergy when he visited a friend who has one. "They called me within forty minutes and said, 'There is really something wrong. You had better come get Charlie.' His eyes had swelled up, and his nose had gotten very congested." And thirteen-year-old Harry finds that if he sleeps overnight at the home of a friend who has a dog, he gets "all stuffed up." As with cats, people may react differently to different breeds of dogs. Katherine "grew up with dogs. We've always had dogs. Never do I remember having any problems." But when she recently got a new bull mastiff, she was soon "sniffling" because she had developed an allergy to it.

It seems as if children can become allergic to just about any furry, hairy or feathered creature with which they come in contact. One three-year-old developed an allergy to the *rabbit* that his baby-sitter kept in a cage in her TV room. Other children become sensitive to *guinea pigs, gerbils* and *hamsters*. Six-year-old Bobby is so highly allergic to *horses* that once when he was eating dinner at a restaurant where horse-and-carriages were going by, "within five minutes, it started," says his mother; "the itchy, watery eyes, the phlegm buildup, the coughing, scratching his head and ears." Children who have little direct exposure to horses can still become allergic to horsehair, which is sometimes used in upholstery, mattresses, carpet padding and insulation.

One woman is so allergic to so many animals, "dogs, cats, everything except goats," she laughs, "that I always enjoy it when my allergist tells me, 'Well, Barbara, you could have a goat as a pet with no problem.' "

OTHER ALLERGENS AND IRRITANTS

Food Less frequently, children can sneeze and have runny noses and watery eyes as the result of an allergy to a food. Two-year-old Margaret, whom we met in Chapter 2, page 17, develops allergic rhinitis whenever she eats bread, cereal, pasta or any other foods that contain wheat. Again, as mentioned in the food allergy chapter, it is not common for rhinitis to be the only symptom of a food allergy.

Occasionally, people who are allergic to ragweed pollen will have itchy and swollen lips, tongues, mouths or throats when they eat watermelon, cantaloupe, honeydew melon or bananas. This is because these foods contain allergenic proteins that are very similar, molecularly, to ragweed allergens.

Irritants Children with allergic rhinitis often also become hypersensitive to a variety of other, nonspecific, irritating substances in the air. Exposure to these irritants then sets off the same symptoms. Among these irritants are:

Tobacco smoke. See Chapter 9, page 158, for a discussion of the effect of parents' smoking on their children's health.

Some components of air pollution: sulfur dioxide, nitrogen oxides, ozone and carbon monoxide.

Automobile exhaust.

Newspaper ink.

Soap and other powders.

Strong smells or fumes of almost any kind—perfume, paint, cooking or food odors.

With Charlie, it's the chalk dust floating in the air in his schoolroom; he makes a point of getting a seat toward the back of the room. With Suzanne, it's often perfume; she finds that using scented tissues to blow her nose is useless because the perfume sets her nose running even more. Sensitivity to such irritants, however, varies enormously from person to person. Some people are severely affected by tobacco smoke, while others say that it does not bother them at all.

WHAT CAUSES ALLERGIC RHINITIS?

If your child has rhinitis due to an allergy to ragweed pollen, it is because his immune system—as we described in Chapter 1, pages 11–13—has made IgE antibodies against ragweed pollen. Similarly, a child who is sensitive to house-dust mites has anti-house-dust-mite IgE antibodies, while a child like Charlie, who is allergic to cat dander, has anti-cat-dander IgE antibodies.

Your child's anti-ragweed-pollen antibodies are on mast cells in the mucous membranes lining his nose. When he inhales a speck of pollen, allergenic molecules in the pollen combine with these antibodies. This causes his mast cells to burst and release histamine and the other biochemical substances, the mediators. These mediators produce his allergic symptoms.

The mediators stimulate nerve endings in his nose, setting off his itching and sneezing. They cause his nasal tissues to secrete more mucus and the blood vessels to dilate and leak fluids, producing the watery discharge from his nose. The mediators also cause his nasal tissues to swell and become inflamed, producing congestion. Over time, they attract white blood cells called eosinophils, as well as other types of white cells, into his nose—greatly amplifying his allergic symptoms.

As a pollen season continues, the membranes lining your child's nose may become more and more sensitive, so that it takes less and less pollen to set off his symptoms. Researchers at Johns Hopkins University have found that toward the end of a season, as little as one hundred grains of ragweed pollen can set some people sneezing. Allergists call this the "priming effect." This priming effect also makes children more sensitive to other allergens; Suzanne notices that during her spring and fall pollen seasons, she itches and sneezes more when she is around her cousin's cat.

As we saw in the section on the symptoms of allergic rhinitis, the common airborne allergens can also affect your child's *eyes.* This is because the mucous membranes of the eyes—which are called the conjunctivas and line the lids and cover the eyeballs—also have mast cells coated with IgE antibodies. When a bit of pollen or other allergen lands on the conjunctiva of an allergic child, it combines with antibodies and causes the release of mediators the same way it does in the nose—causing the eyes to itch and swell and become red and watery. Physicians often use the term "allergic conjunctivitis" for these eye symptoms.

The airborne allergens are also linked with *eczema,* as we saw in Chapter 3, page 41, but their precise contribution to that skin disease is controversial. In some children, pollens can cause the symptoms of eczema to flare—but most people find that their eczema is *better* in the summer, the very time when pollen counts are high. Allergists suspect that exposure to pets and house-dust mites may also play a role in causing some children's eczema to flare. About half of the children who have eczema eventually also develop allergic rhinitis.

Like eczema, allergic rhinitis tends to run in families. About 40 percent of people with the disorder have relatives who also have it. If one parent has allergic rhinitis, it doubles a child's chances of also developing the disorder. If you both have allergic rhinitis, it doubles your child's chances again.

COMPLICATIONS OF ALLERGIC RHINITIS

While allergic rhinitis—in contrast to food allergies—is not life-threatening, it can be far more than just a nuisance for your child, emphasizes Dr. Kravis.

Allergic rhinitis makes children much more vulnerable to *colds and other infections,* both viral and bacterial, of the upper respiratory tract. "An allergic child's nasal airway is not normal," Dr. Kravis explains, "and it therefore doesn't afford the normal protective factors against infections. So your child may have secondary infections superimposed on his allergic rhinitis."

Because the nasal passageways connect with the ears, via the eustachian tubes, children with allergic rhinitis often tend to have recurrent *ear infections*. Their eustachian tubes can be a route for infections to spread from the nose to the ear, and the inflammation and swelling caused by allergic rhinitis can block the normal drainage of secretions from the ear through the tubes into the nasal passages.

Another common complication is *sinusitis*. The sinuses are eight hollow spaces in the head (the word "sinus" means hollow), four on each side surrounding the nose, behind the forehead and the bridge of the nose, and the largest ones, behind the cheeks. The sinuses also secrete mucus, which normally drains into the nasal passages. Sinusitis is simply an inflammation of the sinuses. It usually comes about because the openings of the sinuses have become blocked and the mucus cannot flow out properly, and it is often complicated by an active, local infection. The child may have a congested nose with a colored discharge, a sore throat, bad breath and a persistent cough.

Chronic mouth-breathing may also cause your child to develop *orthodontic problems*. "Breathing through the mouth instead of the nose affects the formation of the jaw," explains Dr. Kravis, "and a child's gums can develop abnormally because they are exposed to the air all of the time, whereas normally the gums would not be so exposed."

While having allergic rhinitis does not make your child more likely to develop *asthma* (see Chapter 7), about 40 percent of children who have allergic rhinitis do also have asthma. And in these children, sinusitis can be an important trigger of acute asthma attacks. "What may happen is that an illness starts out as allergic rhinitis," explains Dr. Kravis. "Then the nasal tissues become secondarily infected, and a sinus infection develops. And that may trigger a child's wheezing. So you may have the lower respiratory tract also involved as a consequence of an allergic reaction that initially was confined to the upper nasal passages."

"While physicians have recognized for years the association between active sinus disease and asthma flare-ups," explains allergist Nicholas A. Pawlowski, M.D., Director of the Allergy Section at The Children's Hospital of Philadelphia, "the precise mechanisms that cause the association are not well understood. However, the key element in treatment is aggressive therapy of the allergy-induced obstruction of the upper airways."

DIAGNOSING ALLERGIC RHINITIS

All children, of course, whether they are allergic or not, have runny or congested noses, red or watery eyes and sneeze from time to time, and there are many possible causes for these symptoms other than allergic rhinitis. Among the other causes, obviously, are *colds and other infections,* both viral and bacterial, of the upper respiratory tract. One tip-off as to whether your child's rhinitis is due to an allergy or an infection is the color of the discharge from his or her nose; a green or yellow nasal discharge is a sign of infection, while the discharge due to allergy is clear and watery. However, a colored discharge does not mean that your child is not allergic; as mentioned above, he or she could easily have *both* an allergy and an infection. "A chronic 'cold' would certainly suggest allergy," points out Dr. Kravis. Colds or infections will usually resolve in a week or two, while a runny nose from allergy goes on and on, as long as a pollen season lasts or the year round.

Some children have noses that run due to certain *physical stimuli,* such as changes in temperature and humidity. Suzanne's nose streams profusely whenever she comes back indoors after she has been outdoors on a very cold winter day. People constantly sympathize, "Do you have a cold?" and it was a long while before she realized that not everyone's nose acts that way.

And many children have trouble breathing through their

nose and must instead breathe through their mouth because they have *enlarged adenoids, nasal polyps* or some *other mechanical obstruction* narrowing or blocking their nasal passageways.

An allergist will pick up clues about whether or not your child is allergic simply by his or her *appearance,* what Dr. Pawlowski calls the "stigmata of allergy." Edward, a handsome young man at the age of seven, has the classic look. His mouth gapes open because his nose is so stuffed up that he must breathe through his mouth, and he also has dark circles under his eyes. Physicians call these "allergic shiners." Allergic children also often have "a little swelling or puffiness on top of their cheeks," explains Dr. Kravis. "The shiners and puffiness tell you that the drainage from their nose is not good and that the blood circulation around their eyes is stagnant." (Children can also have dark circles or puffiness under their eyes for many other reasons—such as not getting enough sleep.) Many allergic children constantly rub and push against their nose, to relieve the characteristic itching and also to open up their nostrils. The "allergic salute," doctors call it. And when physicians look up into an allergic child's nose with their lighted instruments, they can see that the mucous membranes inside are swollen and "bluish or pale rather than reddish," says Dr. Pawlowski, "and we can see the clear discharge."

One of the biggest clues is whether your child's symptoms have a *seasonal pattern,* whether there are times of the year when he or she is better or worse. Recurring rhinitis during the winter months may simply be due to infections. Symptoms that peak during the spring, summer or fall point toward pollen allergies. "If a child has symptoms early in the spring," says Dr. Kravis, "we are, of course, immediately suspicious of the tree pollens. If his symptoms come in the middle of the summer, we suspect the grasses. And if they begin at the end of August and continue into September, we suspect ragweed or some of the other weeds."

Your allergist is also likely to ask you a roster of other questions to ferret out more clues about what specific allergens your child may be encountering in his environment. For example:

Does your family have a cat or a dog or some other pet?

Are there many trees in your neighborhood?

How old is your house or apartment building?

Are there damp places in the basement or elsewhere where molds might flourish?

What kind of heating system does your house have? (Forced-air heat can spew molds and house-dust mites throughout all the rooms of a house.)

Are there any cockroaches in your house or apartment?

Does your child's bedroom have wall-to-wall carpeting? Heavy curtains? Many stuffed animals or books? (These are all dust catchers that can increase a child's exposure to dust mites.)

Does your child use a down pillow or comforter?

Based on your answers to such questions, your allergist will draw up a list of suspect substances that may be causing your child's symptoms.

Skin Tests The key test that allergists use for diagnosing nasal allergies is the skin test, which—as we have seen in Chapters 2 and 3—they also use for detecting food and skin allergies. In this procedure, a nurse or doctor places drops of extracts of each suspect substance on your child's skin. If your child is allergic to cats, for example, and has anti-cat IgE antibodies, his skin will show a visible reaction to cat extract. See Chapter 8, pages 125–28, for more details about how allergists perform skin tests, what they show and their possible side effects.

When five-year-old Caroline, whose symptoms run from March through June, first visited her allergist, the doctor decided—on the basis of her mother's answers to questions—to skin test Caroline for forty-five different allergens, including a number of tree, grass and weed pollens, house-dust mites and four kinds of molds. But because Caroline has no contact with cats, dogs or other animals, she did not test her for their allergens. Caroline turned out to have positive skin tests to the pollens of birch, maple, ash, beech, hickory and poplar trees—but, curiously, *not* to pollens from some equally common trees: oak, elm, sycamore, cedar, mulberry and sweet gum. "She may be more exposed to the first ones in the area where she lives," notes Dr. Kravis. Of the grasses, Caroline reacted positively to the pollens of two (June and orchard) but not to timothy or fescue, nor was she sensitive to any of the weeds (including ragweed) or molds. She is also allergic to house-dust mites.

Six-year-old Jimmy, on the other hand—out of twenty-eight skin tests—turned out to be allergic only to two tree pollens (ash and oak), cockroaches and house-dust mites. Jimmy was delighted to learn that he is *not* allergic to cats; he hopes that his mother will now get him the two Siamese he wants. Since Jimmy clearly has an allergic tendency, however, "he may become sensitive to cats," Dr. Pawlowski warns, *"after* he is exposed to them."

Testing the Nose, Ears and Lungs To find out whether your child's sinuses are infected or whether he has enlarged adenoids or some other obstruction blocking his nasal airways, physicians may order *X-ray studies* of his head and neck.

Doctors often test a child's ears with an instrument called a *tympanometer*. They place an earpiece against the child's eardrum; the device generates a gentle (and painless) pressure, measures the eardrum's compliance (mobility) and then prints out a curve on graph paper. "The shape of this curve gives us an idea whether there is fluid in the middle ear," explains Dr. Kravis. "There shouldn't be, but it does often happen in atopic children."

And to find out whether a child's cough is due, at least in

part, to asthma, the doctors perform *spirometry* to assess how well his or her lungs are working. See Chapter 7, pages 109–110, for more information about spirometry and other ways of testing children's lungs.

Laboratory Tests There are also several kinds of laboratory tests that your allergist may order.

Sometimes physicians take a sample of a child's nasal secretions by having him blow his nose onto a special paper. Then they smear the secretions on a microscope slide and have the lab count the numbers of eosinophils (page 68) and other types of white cells on the slide. This is called *nasal cytology*. "This is a simple test," says Dr. Kravis, "and sometimes when we don't know if a child's rhinitis is allergic or not, this test may clinch the diagnosis if more than 20 percent of the cells are eosinophils."

The physicians may also test a child's blood for its overall level of *IgE antibodies* or for IgE antibodies specifically against particular allergens.

Allergists sometimes have parents take home with them *"mold plates,"* plastic dishes containing a special gel on which molds grow readily. You expose the dishes for half an hour to the air in the rooms that you suspect may be mold-infested and then, if mold growth appears on the gel within five days, you take the dishes back to your allergist for laboratory identification.

TREATING ALLERGIC RHINITIS

Avoiding Allergens The number-one treatment for allergic rhinitis—as it is for other allergies—is to try to prevent it: that is, for your child to avoid, if at all possible, whatever allergens are producing his or her symptoms. "If one is able to define the cause," emphasizes Dr. Kravis, "the best treatment is removal."

If your child turns out to be allergic to your cat, dog or other animal, this is a fairly straightforward thing to accomplish. "Then the solution is pretty obvious," says Dr. Kravis. The best thing to do, allergists advise, is for you to get rid of the pet and for your child to stay away from other people's animals.

If your child is allergic to pollens or to molds or house-dust mites, which are plentiful in so many houses, there are many measures that you can take at home to reduce their levels.

See Chapter 9, pages 151–58, for practical tips on how you can minimize your child's exposure to animal danders and other airborne allergens.

Medications In contrast to the situation with food allergies, there are many medications that—singly or in combinations—can help to prevent or to control symptoms of allergic rhinitis in most children. "We can always do something," says Dr. Kravis, "to relieve or minimize a child's degree of discomfort."

The drugs that physicians most frequently prescribe for allergic rhinitis are the *antihistamines,* which, as we have seen, they also use for food and skin allergies. Antihistamines act relatively quickly: within a half-hour or so, usually, they reduce sneezing, itching and the runny discharge from a child's nose. Antihistamines are less effective, however, at relieving nasal congestion. For that, doctors often suggest *decongestants,* which reduce swelling and open up nasal passages by causing the blood vessels in the nose to constrict.

There are now also two newer categories of medications—*cromolyn* and *corticosteroids*—that a child uses topically; that is, he or she sprays them directly inside the nose. Unlike antihistamines and decongestants, cromolyn and the topical corticosteroids do not work quickly but are both preventatives. "You need to use them for at least two to three weeks," explains Dr. Sweinberg, "before they achieve their maximum effectiveness."

Like antihistamines, cromolyn is better at reducing sneezing, itching and runny noses than it is at relieving congestion.

The topical corticosteroids reduce swelling and inflammation in the nose and also help block the allergic reaction from occurring in the first place. See Chapter 8, pages 129–32 and pages 137–41, for more detailed information about these medications, their modes of actions, what they can and cannot do and their possible side effects.

Just which combination of drugs a physician will prescribe for a given child "is an individual sort of thing based on the severity of a child's symptoms," points out Dr. Sweinberg. "Every child is different.

"A younger child, or a child with only mild symptoms, we treat symptomatically; that is, we wait until his or her symptoms appear. Even though your child is allergic to ragweed, it doesn't mean that he or she is automatically going to have symptoms as soon as ragweed season starts. What we do is give parents a medication, usually just an antihistamine, so that they have it on hand when the child does need it. And oftentimes we rely on the parents to help us decide whether a child needs it three times a day or just once, at bedtime.

"In older children, we tend more to use antihistamine-decongestant combinations." Antihistamines may make a child drowsy, while decongestants may stimulate him. "The nice thing is that the side effects counteract each other, so most children do well. The frequency, again, the parents could help decide. We might tell them a maximum of two to three times a day, if the symptoms are severe. Sometimes a child can get away with just a once-a-day dosing and get protection for a full twenty-four-hour period."

Decongestants also come in the form of nasal sprays, but physicians warn against using such topical decongestants for any length of time. "What happens is that they work only briefly," Dr. Sweinberg continues, "and then you get a 're-bound effect,' and they actually make the nose *more* congested. People use them more and more often and become dependent on them. It's called 'rhinitis medicamentosa.' If a child is really very severely obstructed, I will recommend one for three to five days only. I don't like to use it any longer than that, and I always make sure that the parents are aware of the potential danger.

"Then there is the other child who, every year, the parents know that come August 15, say, will have problems. This child you may want to start on nasal steroids or cromolyn a week or two before the season hits, to get his nose in really good condition so that when the pollens are present, he does not have all the mediators released." Once his symptoms start, the child would probably also take antihistamines.

Some children with severe allergic rhinitis take all four of these medications—antihistamine, decongestant, nasal cromolyn *and* nasal corticosteroid—and some with year-round allergies take all four throughout the entire year.

The antihistamines that a child takes by mouth for nasal symptoms often also relieve his or her eye symptoms. However, there are also topical, ophthalmic versions of antihistamines, cromolyn and corticosteroids—in the form of eye drops—that physicians sometimes prescribe for allergic conjunctivitis. The corticosteroid drops, however, can cause serious complications in the eyes and, Dr. Pawlowski emphasizes, are used *only* when a person has *extremely severe* symptoms.

Allergy Shots If these drugs do not control your child's symptoms well enough or cause bothersome side effects, allergists may recommend a course of *immunotherapy*—what most people call *allergy shots*. "First, we try elimination, avoidance of the allergens," says Dr. Kravis, "and then symptomatic treatment and then, if that fails, those patients eventually go on to receive immunotherapy. It all depends on how severe a child's problem is and what his response is to these other measures." Adds Dr. Sweinberg, "We first try medications for a good six months."

Allergists are more likely to suggest immunotherapy for

children with year-round allergies or for those who are allergic to many pollens. "If a child has pollen problems confined to the ragweed season, which may be just six weeks," Dr. Kravis continues, "you do everything you can to work with medications, because six weeks is not a long time to be uncomfortable."

Allergists more often give shots to older children than to younger ones. "We do try to defer these injections in a small child," says Dr. Kravis, "unless we have our backs against the wall. We've tried everything else, and nothing has worked. I always try to hold off as long as possible." Allergists are even more likely to give shots to adults than to children. "Children put up with more," notes Dr. Sweinberg. "They can't verbalize their discomfort." Adults may find that their symptoms are interfering with their work and with driving a car, and "some adults are very sensitive to the sedative effect of the antihistamines."

Five-year-old Caroline is now taking allergy shots because her symptoms were "very, very severe," explains her mother. "Every year, they just kept getting progressively worse. By last spring, her eyes were so swollen that they were just two slits. You couldn't even see her eyes. And her nose was so congested that many times she couldn't breathe through it at all." She was constantly getting sinusitis and ear infections, secondary to the allergies, and "she was taking so much antihistamine that she was sleeping fifteen hours a day and it was hard to rouse her. This was no way for a little kid to live."

Unlike immunization shots against infectious diseases, with allergy shots allergists must first tailor-make—specifically for each child—a mixture of dilute extracts of the substances to which he or she is allergic. The "recipe" for Caroline's injections calls for extracts of the allergens her skin tests showed that she is sensitive to: house-dust mites and pollens from birch, ash, beech, hickory, maple and poplar trees and June and orchard grasses.

Children must take allergy shots every week, or sometimes

every two weeks, for at least three years, and "it takes between six months and a year to see a response," says Dr. Sweinberg. Immunotherapy, like drugs, may produce side effects, and it does not always work for everyone. See Chapter 8, pages 141–45, for more about when and how doctors give allergy shots, how they work and their risks and limitations.

Caroline has now been taking allergy shots every week for over nine months, and for her, they are already working well. "The shots have been a miraculous help," says her mother, "because I don't have to overly medicate her, and she can function. And she is not getting the secondary things, the sinusitis or the ear problems, at all. It's a wonderful, wonderful thing."

What Happens as a Child Grows

In contrast to food allergies and eczema, which children often outgrow, allergic rhinitis usually does tend to persist as a lifelong affliction. "Very often, allergic rhinitis continues all through a person's adulthood," notes Dr. Kravis.

However, the severity of a person's symptoms often varies from time to time. Some people find that their symptoms get better as they grow older; others find that they get worse, and the symptoms often change as a person changes environments and is exposed to different allergens. One grown-up, for instance, developed an allergy to tree pollens, for the first time, when she moved from the city to the suburbs. Another found that her allergy to molds lessened when she moved from Iowa to the high, dry plains of Colorado.

Fortunately, the medications and immunotherapy can help almost everyone with allergic rhinitis. There are people who take allergy shots well into their seventies and eighties. One New York businessman, for instance, has been taking them for twenty-eight years—but needs no drugs and has no symptoms, no side effects from the shots and no problem. "The shots work just fine," he reports.

CHAPTER 5

Allergies to Insect Stings

Many children are allergic to fragments of insects—particularly those of house-dust mites and cockroaches—that they inhale with the air they breathe, as we saw in the previous chapter on allergic rhinitis. Children can also, less commonly, become allergic to the venom of certain insects that sting. Unlike allergies to inhaled insect fragments, allergies to the venoms of these stinging insects can sometimes be life-threatening.

Nearly 2 million Americans each year, according to the National Institute of Allergy and Infectious Diseases, suffer from allergic reactions to stinging-insect venoms. In one survey of nearly five thousand Boy Scouts, ages eleven to sixteen, who were attending a summer camp in Rhode Island, twenty of them—0.4 percent—were allergic to insect venoms.

The Stinging Insects

All of the insects that can sting belong to a group that entomologists call the Hymenoptera (from the Greek for "membrane-winged"), which includes the bees, wasps, hornets and ants. Only the females sting: at the tips of their abdomens they have stingers that resemble miniature hypodermic needles. They pierce our flesh and then inject their venoms from special venom sacs that are located at the base of their stingers.

Bees   Among the bees, the smaller, brown *honeybees* are more aggressive and quicker to sting us humans than are the larger, black-and-yellow *bumblebees,* which tend to mind their own business of collecting pollen to feed their larvae. Honeybees sting to protect both themselves and their hives, and they can do so only once, because they die in the act. Their stingers are barbed in such a way that they cannot withdraw them from their victim's wound without fatally injuring themselves.

Wasps and Hornets   Wasps and hornets, on the other hand, can sting again and again, and they do so both to defend themselves and also to kill other insects as food for their larvae. The yellow-and-black-striped *yellow jackets,* in particular, are notoriously nasty-tempered and apt to attack us even without any apparent provocation. "I was simply dozing in the backyard on a late summer day," says Marjorie, "just lying there, and I felt this sharp sting on my left hand." Another girl was simply walking down the street when a yellow jacket zapped her on the knuckle of her third finger. Other perpetrators include the common *white-faced hornets* (sometimes called bald-faced hornets), which are black with light markings, the *yellow hornets* and the *Polistes paper wasps,* which get their name because they fashion their nests out of a paperlike material that they manufacture by chewing up bark.

Ants   Among the ants, the stings of *harvester ants* occasionally cause allergic reactions, but the real villains are *imported fire ants,* which in recent years have invaded the southeastern United States from South America in great numbers. There are two species—the red *Solenopsis invicta,* native to

Brazil, Argentina and Paraguay, and the black *Solenopsis richteri,* native to Argentina and Uruguay—and they both seem to have entered this country early in this century aboard cargo ships unloading at the Gulf Coast port of Mobile, Alabama. Today, the fire ants have spread eastward to Florida, as far west as Texas and as far north as North Carolina, Tennessee, Arkansas and Oklahoma, and they are now threatening to move even farther west into New Mexico and California.

Imported fire ants live in colonies consisting of hundreds of thousands of individuals, and they construct unsightly mounds, a foot or more in height, that litter lawns, parks and farmer's fields, in some places as densely as two hundred mounds to an acre. These imported fire ants have become serious agricultural pests. They destroy crops and damage farm machinery that unexpectedly hits their mounds, and they have proved extraordinarily resistant to pesticides and other means of eradication.

When these imported fire ants sting, they first bite a person and get a good grip with their mouth parts; then they arch their abdomens and swivel around to sting their victims repeatedly in a circular pattern. They manage to sting some 30 to 60 percent of the population in the afflicted states each year, more often children than adults.

Biting Insects   Some people also occasionally suffer allergic reactions to the saliva of certain insects that bite, rather than sting. These include *mosquitoes, black flies,* some *midges, deer flies, bedbugs, fleas* and *kissing bugs.* Mosquitoes, in contrast to the hymenoptera (which sting us to defend themselves), bite us because they must feed on the blood of warm-blooded animals. Kissing bugs, which live in the Southern part of the United States, get their name because they inflict multiple bites, up to fifteen at a feeding, clustered on an exposed arm, leg or face.

THE SYMPTOMS OF INSECT-STING ALLERGIES

If your child is *not* allergic to the venom of a particular insect, his or her reaction to a sting will usually be some mild pain, redness and swelling that is confined to the site of the sting and disappears within a few hours.

In a child who *is* allergic to any venom, the most common symptoms are hives and the tissue swelling called angio-edema (see Chapter 3, pages 47–51). These reactions can range from a single large hive, a single wheal-and-flare, at the site of the sting, to hives all over the child's body and dramatic swelling of his or her tissues. Fire-ant stings usually also cause an immediate severe burning sensation at the sting site and intense itching that may last for days.

The swelling is often on an extremity, notes Dr. Steven M. Selbst, Director of the Emergency Department at The Children's Hospital of Philadelphia. "The child may get stung on the hands, or the nose, or ears or around the eyes, and the tendency is for the tissue to really blow up. The whole hand is swollen and may look terrible, all puffy and red. Or the whole side of the child's face, around the eye, swells up, and the child can't even open his eye."

When the yellow jacket stung Marjorie in her own backyard, "before I knew it," she reports, "my hand swelled up to the size of a boxing glove. I couldn't believe it." The following day her hand was still swollen so much that she could not bend her fingers well enough to pick up anything at all. "It was not a useful hand. It was very squishy."

Like food allergies, an allergic reaction to insect venom can threaten a child's life if it causes the tissues around the larynx to swell so much that he or she has trouble breathing. When Marjorie telephoned her allergist about the yellow-jacket sting on her hand, she recalls, "His cheerful question was: 'Is your throat closing up?' I said, 'No.'"

An insect sting can also be life-threatening by causing the body-wide allergic reaction called anaphylaxis (see Chapter

2, pages 16–17): the person's blood pressure may drop and his heart beat irregularly, and he may become unconscious and go into shock. Some forty people each year in the United States die, studies show, from such allergic reactions to insect venoms. And in the years since the South American fire ants invaded this country, allergic reactions to their venom have killed at least eighty-four people.

"However, those deaths are in all age groups," points out allergist Lillian P. Kravis, M.D., of The Children's Hospital of Philadelphia. "Most of those are not in children. Fatalities in the pediatric age group are so very, very rare that I have never seen even one. You have to do an intensive search in the medical literature to come up with a case. Parents should be aware of the possibility, certainly, but they should not be frightened to death by it.

"There is something very interesting about insect-sting allergies in children," Dr. Kravis continues, "and that is, it is very common for a child to react with generalized hives on one occasion and have no allergic reaction whatsoever on the next occasion. There is a variability in children's reactions, which we cannot explain."

Allergic reactions to the saliva of some of the biting insects can, on rare occasions, also cause anaphylactic shock, but the biting insects tend to produce much less severe symptoms than do the stinging insects, and also fewer people are allergic to them.

WHAT CAUSES INSECT-STING ALLERGIES?

As with allergies to foods and to inhaled substances, if your child is allergic to the venom of a stinging insect, it is because his immune system has made IgE antibodies (see Chapter 1, pages 11–12) specifically against that venom. Marjorie, for example, has IgE antibodies against yellow-jacket venom in her body, while a child allergic to honeybee stings has IgE antibodies against honeybee venom.

When Marjorie was stung, allergenic molecules in the venom combined with these anti-yellow-jacket antibodies, which are on mast cells in her skin, blood and other tissues. This caused the mast cells to release histamine and the other biochemical substances, the mediators, that produced her allergic symptoms. There is some cross-reactivity between the venoms of some of these insects; if your child is allergic to one of these venoms, he or she may also be allergic to some of the others.

DIAGNOSING INSECT-STING ALLERGIES

You sometimes know when your child has been stung by an insect, but "very often parents don't know," says Dr. Selbst. Hives and swelling due to an insect sting can look just like hives and swelling from any other cause. "The important thing that we have to do is to distinguish it from an infection. Insect bites are not tender and are not associated with a fever, as are infections. Among other things, we look to see if we can find a small area where there is definitely a sting."

Parents frequently do not know which particular insect was responsible for a sting. One insect that doctors can sometimes identify after the fact is the honeybee, because it may leave its stinger in the wound.

Skin Tests To identify the specific insect venoms to which your child may be sensitive, allergists can perform skin tests using venom extracts. These tests show whether your child has IgE antibodies in his or her skin against particular venoms.

In 1979 the Food and Drug Administration approved venom extracts for five hymenoptera: honeybee, yellow jacket, yellow hornet, white-faced hornet and the *Polistes* paper wasp. At this time, extracts of imported fire-ant venom are not available; allergists skin test children for fire-ant allergy using extracts made not just from venom but from whole fire-ant bodies.

See Chapter 8, pages 126–29, for more about skin tests, how allergists perform them, what they mean and their possible side effects.

TREATING INSECT-STING ALLERGIES

Medications If your child suffers an allergic reaction—hives, angioedema or anaphylaxis—due to an insect sting, physicians treat him or her the same way that they would treat him for these symptoms due to an allergic reaction to food: *antihistamines* by mouth to reduce the itching, *corticosteroids* by mouth to reduce inflammation and sometimes an injection of *epinephrine (adrenaline)*. (See Chapter 8, pages 129–30 and 135–41, for a discussion of these medications, what they accomplish and their possible side effects.) When Marjorie's left hand blew up like a boxing glove after she was stung by a yellow jacket, her allergist prescribed both antihistamines and corticosteroids. For life-threatening anaphylaxis, physicians may also administer oxygen, intravenous fluids and still other medications.

Physicians advise parents of a child who reacts to insect venom with generalized, body-wide hives to carry with them, whenever they might encounter a stinging insect, both antihistamines and a kit containing a prefilled syringe of epinephrine. "I now keep one in the kitchen," says Marjorie, "and I carry one to the beach and any place I go where there are liable to be bugs." Since children's allergic reactions to stings are so variable, however, "the chances are," says Dr. Kravis, "that you are not going to have to use the kit. Your child's next episode can be one single hive or nothing at all."

Physicians also recommend that a child highly allergic to insect stings wear a necklace or bracelet with a tag describing the allergy and telling whom to contact in case of an emergency. At Marjorie's school, the nurse keeps a careful list of all the students who are allergic to these stinging-insect venoms.

Allergy Shots As with allergies to pollens and other inhaled allergens, allergists can desensitize a person to insect venom by administering venom immunotherapy, a series of shots containing insect–venom extracts. The physicians can do this for the five hymenoptera for which venom extracts are available: honeybee, yellow jacket, yellow hornet, white-faced hornet and the *Polistes* paper wasp. For allergies to imported fire ants, doctors give shots using extracts not just of venom but of whole fire-ant bodies. See Chapter 8, pages 141–45, for more about allergy shots, how they are given, how they work and their possible side effects.

Because children's allergic reactions to insects are so variable, "we treat children very differently from adults," Dr. Kravis explains. "Whereas in adults, generalized hives and swelling would be an indication for allergy shots, in children that is not the case. Unless a child develops trouble breathing or shock, we would not desensitize a child."

Preventing Insect Stings As with all allergies, prevention is the best treatment for allergies to insect stings. If you have a child who experiences severe reactions to venoms, you should become familiar with the habits of the stinging insects prevalent in your area and teach your child how to avoid them. Many of these insects are attracted by food and drink. In the Philadelphia area, yellow jackets, in particular, show up in the summer as uninvited guests, during daylight hours, at picnics and cookouts. Covering leftover food and garbage helps discourage them. Perfume, suntan creams and aromatic cosmetics also attract many of these insects. Since some of them make their nests in the ground, Marjorie's allergist advised her, "Never go out in your backyard without wearing shoes." Long-sleeved shirts and long pants can also reduce the area of your child's skin exposed to a possible attack. And obviously, if you have any stinging-insect nests on your own property, you should get rid of them.

CHAPTER 6

Allergies to Drugs

Anytime that anyone, child or adult, takes any medication, there is some—relatively small—risk of an adverse reaction. All drugs can on occasion produce unwanted side effects, and some people have idiosyncratic reactions to drugs that cause no problems for others. Fortunately, most of these reactions are minor and transient. Some 6 to 25 percent of all adverse effects from medications, according to various estimates, are due to true, allergic reactions to the drugs.

These allergic drug reactions occur more frequently in adults than children, presumably because adults have had more cumulative exposures to more kinds of drugs. Yet "they are not an uncommon kind of problem for a number of children," says Dr. Nicholas A. Pawlowski, Director of the Allergy Section at The Children's Hospital of Philadelphia. "They can cause trouble at repeated intervals, over time, and they create a lot of anxiety among parents."

The likelihood of a drug causing an allergic reaction varies with its route of administration. A child is most likely to develop an allergy to a medication applied directly to his or her skin; see the section discussing contact dermatitis in Chapter

3, pages 51–56. A child is *least* likely to become allergic to a drug that he or she takes by mouth, and a drug that is injected is more likely to cause an allergic reaction than one taken orally.

THE SYMPTOMS OF DRUG ALLERGY

Whatever the route, the most common allergic reactions to drugs show up on the skin: they cause rashes, itching, hives and the dramatic swelling known as angioedema (see Chapter 3, pages 47–51).

When five-year-old Geoffrey was taking a sulfa antibiotic recently, for example, he suddenly developed hives "from head to toe," reports his mother. "Some were the size of silver dollars, and he itched all over. His hands puffed up to the size of his father's; they were like big red lobsters."

Occasionally, allergic reactions to drugs can produce the life-threatening condition called anaphylaxis (see Chapter 2, pages 16–17), which can also be caused by allergies to foods and to the venoms of stinging insects.

THE DRUGS COMMONLY CAUSING ALLERGIES

Of all the many categories of drugs, the *antibiotics*—particularly *penicillin* and its relatives—are responsible for the largest number of allergic reactions in both children and adults. "The broad group of penicillin-type antibiotics are the most common causes in children. The reason is a combination of two factors," explains Dr. Pawlowski. "First, there is probably something about the penicillin molecule that makes it particularly allergenic, and second, there is also the matter of exposure. Children take a lot of this type of antibiotic for infections."

Among the many other categories of drugs that can cause allergic reactions in children are *insulin, anticonvulsants, anesthetics, tetanus toxoid* and *other vaccines*. In some cases, "it may not be the vaccine itself that is allergenic," explains allergist Sharon K. Sweinberg, M.D., of The Children's Hospital of Philadelphia, "but constituents in it, such as egg or neomycin." Diabetic children can develop antibodies to secondary ingredients in insulin preparations and also to the insulin molecule itself, which the immune system recognizes as a foreign protein invading the body from outside. "Insulin allergy is not an uncommon problem," says Dr. Pawlowski, "nor are reactions to anesthetics, both local and general. However, it is exceptionally rare that a child has an immediate, IgE-type reaction to anticonvulsants. It happens here at this hospital no more than once or twice a year."

In children who are allergic to penicillin, their immune systems have formed IgE antibodies—the same sort of antibodies responsible for allergies to foods, inhaled substances and stinging-insect venoms—specifically against penicillin molecules. These children have anti-penicillin antibodies attached to mast cells in their bodies. When penicillin molecules combine with the antibodies, the mast cells burst and release histamine and the other biochemical substances, the mediators, that produce the allergic symptoms.

"These IgE reactions," says Dr. Pawlowski, "are the ones that cause some of the worst drug reactions, and they usually occur within the first four hours of taking the drug." Anaphylactic reactions to penicillin may kill, it is estimated, four hundred to eight hundred people a year in the United States, far more than anaphylaxis due to any other cause. Virtually all these deaths occur after the drug has been injected, rather than taken by mouth, and most occur in adults in their twenties, thirties and forties. However, they can occur in infants and children, although "we really don't see fatalities in children in significant numbers," says allergist Lillian P. Kravis, M.D., of The Children's Hospital of Philadelphia.

Penicillins and other drugs can also, less commonly, cause adverse reactions in both children and adults by means of other immune mechanisms that do not involve IgE antibodies. Sometimes another type of antibody—IgG antibodies (see Chapter 1, page 11)—combines with drug molecules coating red blood cells, destroying the blood cells and producing anemia. Or complexes of drug molecules combined with antibodies may become deposited in body tissues, producing serum sickness or kidney disease. Some of these other immune mechanisms can also cause life-threatening reactions, but these are extremely rare.

"We really don't understand these other mechanisms well enough yet," says Dr. Pawlowski. "There are still many reactions to drugs that are confusing. Many are manifested as rashes. For example, ampicillin by itself can cause a rash that takes a longer time to develop than the IgE reactions. It is common in children. Viruses alone can cause rashes, and some rashes—this is more rare—may truly be due to a combination of reactions to a drug and to a virus. Patients with infectious mononucleosis who are taking ampicillin can get a vicious, vicious rash."

DIAGNOSING DRUG ALLERGIES

A problem physicians have in diagnosing allergies to medications is that the most common symptoms—rashes, itching, hives, angioedema—are not unique to drug allergies. These symptoms can be produced by many conditions, including, often, the disease for which the child is taking the drug. When Geoffrey showed up at The Children's Hospital of Philadelphia with his silver-dollar hives and red-lobster hands, Dr. Jack Becker explained to his parents that Geoffrey's virus infection itself could well be causing this reaction.

Geoffrey's hives and swelling had started shortly after dinner one night, after he had been taking the sulfa for twenty days, and they continued off and on for three days. Dr. Becker carefully queried his parents about whether the boy had eaten any new foods. Geoffrey had indeed eaten a different brand of tuna fish; he had remarked on its taste and then eaten only four bites. "Four bites of tuna could cause this reaction," Dr. Becker explained, "but it wouldn't continue for three days."

An allergic reaction to the sulfa that Geoffrey was taking for his infection could also cause these symptoms, Dr. Becker continued, but it was unusual that the reaction would start on day twenty of his drug therapy. "Usually you see an allergic reaction, involving IgE antibodies, right away, but it may have taken his immune system this long to build up the antibodies. The likelihood is that his hives and angioedema are due to an allergic reaction to the sulfa. There is maybe a 60 percent probability that they are due to the drug."

Skin Tests Allergists can skin test (see Chapter 8, pages 125–29) a child for IgE antibodies for some drugs, but among the antibiotics, doctors can skin test only for penicillin. The necessary extracts for the others are not available. However, allergists test children for penicillin allergy only when they need the drug. "We don't test ex post facto," explains Dr. Pawlowski. "We commonly have patients referred for testing a month *after* they have had some sort of reaction to penicillin. That is not advisable for two reasons.

"One is that if the child did have an allergic reaction, he could have a false negative reaction on the test because his IgE antibodies are used up. Second, there is harm that can be done in skin testing. If a child is truly allergic to penicillin, what we are doing is boosting his body's production of IgE antibodies to it. So we skin test for penicillin just before we intend to start it, as part of making the decision whether to start it. We tell these parents to bring the child back for skin testing if and when he really needs penicillin."

"A lot of children are labeled penicillin-allergic," notes Dr. Kravis, "when, in fact, they are not, because they reacted in infancy and the distinction wasn't made as to whether the rash was due to the drug or to the viral illness. So we are often asked to sort out that problem: is this patient really allergic to penicillin?"

One child whose possible drug allergy was sorted out recently by the allergists at The Children's Hospital of Philadelphia was three-year-old Christina. Since Christina had started going to a day-care center four months earlier, she had had frequent infections of her upper respiratory tract and also her ears. She had had several courses of penicillin, and during one course, she developed very itchy hives all over her body. Her pediatrician then switched her to a sulfa antibiotic, but after one dose, she again developed hives.

Since Christina clearly needed an antibiotic, The Children's Hospital allergists decided that they should skin test her. She did indeed turn out to test positive for penicillin allergy. "Because we can't test for sulfa," added Dr. Kravis, "we ought to assume that she is allergic to sulfa drugs too."

TREATING DRUG ALLERGIES

The first step that doctors take in treating a child for an allergic reaction to a drug is to stop administering the drug. When Geoffrey's parents brought him to the Emergency Department at The Children's Hospital of Philadelphia for his hives and swelling, the physicians told his parents to stop giving him the sulfa. And when Christina's mother told her pediatrician about her hives, the doctor had her discontinue both the sulfa and the penicillin.

Medications Next, doctors treat hives and angioedema due to drug allergy the same way as when they are due to allergic reactions to a food or insect venom: the physicians usually suggest _antihistamines_ and they may inject _epinephrine (adrenaline)_ or prescribe oral _corticosteroids_. (See Chapter 8, pages 129–30 and pages 135–41, for more information about these drugs.)

Geoffrey's doctors gave him antihistamines, three shots of epinephrine over a two-day period, and then when he still had some symptoms also had him take corticosteroids. And both times that Christina had hives, from penicillin and then from sulfa, her pediatrician prescribed antihistamines.

If the child still needs medication for his or her original illness, the next step is to administer alternative drugs. Fortunately, says Dr. Kravis, "there are now many alternatives to penicillin." When Christina's skin test showed that she was allergic to penicillin, and, by assumption, to sulfa drugs also, Dr. Kravis suggested that she could instead take erythromycin or one of the newer cephalosporins as an alternative antibiotic for her recurring ear infections.

To prevent allergic reactions to drugs, physicians routinely ask parents whether a child has ever had any adverse reactions to any medications. And whenever the physicians in the Emergency Department at The Children's Hospital of Philadelphia give an injection of penicillin, "we take precautions about it," says Dr. Steven M. Selbst, Director of the Emergency Department. Whether or not the child has ever had a reaction to the drug, "we keep him around for fifteen minutes or so to look out for an allergic reaction." A reaction to a shot would be immediate: if the child does have one, the physicians can treat it promptly to keep it from developing into a serious problem. "But I don't think we've seen a reaction to a penicillin shot in a couple of years."

"We are often faced with the following situation," adds Dr. Pawlowski. "A child has had a serious allergic reaction to penicillin in the past and now really needs a course of oral penicillin. We perform skin tests. If in our judgment he is going to be just fine, we still will give him a test dose in the hospital, as an outpatient. We will ask the parent and child to hang around, have lunch, play in the atrium, which is right next to the emergency room, and we will observe the child for four hours in case of that extremely rare occurrence."

If a child who is clearly allergic to a drug does need that particular drug, physicians have still other ways of dealing with the situation. "In a life-threatening situation," says Dr.

Pawlowski, "if a child is in the hospital with an infection of the heart or meningitis or a deep-tissue infection, and needs immediate antibiotics, we can desensitize the child." The doctors administer very tiny doses of the drug—starting with as little as one ten-thousandth of the usual dose—at frequent intervals, gradually increasing the dose over a period of hours or days, until they work up to a full therapeutic dose.

If any of your children have had allergic reactions to any medication, you should not only remember the name of the drug but also make note of other relevant details. "We commonly have the situation," explains Dr. Pawlowski, "where a child has had a rash with a penicillin antibiotic at some time in the past, and the parents say that they were told never to give him the drug again. The problem is that often there are no precise records of what happened. What needs to be carefully documented is the timing of the rash—that is, when the rash broke out in relationship to the beginning of the drug therapy—and what kind of rash it was, what it looked like and also its distribution on the child's body." Parents should write down these details at the time so they can give this information to other physicians in the future. "It would prevent a lot of confusion."

Physicians sometimes recommend that children who are allergic to specific drugs wear a necklace or a bracelet with a tag describing their sensitivity—just as do some children who have allergies to foods and to stinging-insect venoms.

CHAPTER 7

Asthma

The lung disease asthma is the most common chronic disease that afflicts children. In the United States 3 million children under the age of eighteen—more than 7 percent of all children—suffer from it, according to the National Heart, Lung and Blood Institute. All together, 10 million Americans have the disease.

Asthma is by far the most serious and the most complex of all the allergic disorders because it is chronic and affects so many children and because it can be life-threatening. Asthma is responsible for 163,000 admissions of children to hospitals each year, and at The Children's Hospital of Philadelphia, it accounts for 1,300 admissions a year, nearly 9 percent of all admissions—an average of 3 or 4 children every day.

Over the past ten years, however, there have been so many improvements in diagnosing and treating asthma, that "today most children who have asthma," says Dr. Nicholas A. Pawlowski, Director of the Allergy Section at The Children's Hospital of Philadelphia, "should be able to live with virtually no limitations on their lifestyles."

In 1991, the Heart, Lung Institute's National Asthma Education Program released a comprehensive Expert Panel Report entitled *Guidelines for the Diagnosis and Management of Asthma,* which represents the current consensus of asthma specialists in this country. This Expert Panel Report, too, emphasizes that asthma is a treatable disease and that with an accurate diagnosis and appropriate treatment, most people who have asthma can expect to lead normal, active lives.

Nevertheless, this Expert Panel Report stresses, asthma is frequently underdiagnosed, particularly in children. And, adds Dr. Pawlowski, "It is also still all too common for children with asthma to receive inadequate care and follow-up."

THE SYMPTOMS: WHAT HAPPENS DURING AN ASTHMA ATTACK

Children (and grown-ups) who have asthma suffer periodic episodes when the airways of their lungs become obstructed and they have difficulty in breathing. This is because they have twitchy airways; that is, their airways are hyperresponsive to various stimuli or triggers (see pages 102–06) that do not affect children with normal lungs.

Our lungs are shaped somewhat like an upside-down tree. When we breathe in, air flows down through our trachea (our windpipe), the trunk of the tree. In the chest, the trachea branches into two bronchial tubes, which direct the air toward the right and left lungs. The bronchial tubes, in turn, branch and rebranch into smaller air passageways, called bronchi, and even smaller ones, called bronchioles. These are the twigs of the tree. At the tips of the bronchioles are the air sacs, which are also called alveoli. These are the leaves of the tree. It is across the membranes of these air sacs that our blood picks up the oxygen we need from the air and gets rid of the waste gas, carbon dioxide.

When a child who has asthma suffers an acute episode, the muscles surrounding his or her air passageways, including the tiniest bronchi and bronchioles, go into spasm and contract, reducing the diameter of these airways. "An asthmatic's airways react more—that is, the bronchial muscles constrict more—in response to a given trigger than do normal airways," explains Dr. Pawlowski. "This characteristic has led to an alternative name for asthma: *reactive airway disease.*"

During such asthma attacks, the mucous membranes lining the child's airways also swell and become inflamed, thus narrowing these air tubes even more. These membranes also secrete excessive amounts of thick mucus, which clogs the breathing tubes and further interferes with the flow of air in and out of the lungs.

This inflammation of the airways, physicians have increasingly come to realize, is a key component of asthma. Traditionally, the Heart, Lung Institute's Expert Panel Report points out, doctors have considered the constriction of the bronchial muscles the primary feature of asthma. "We now know that inflammation is the predominant feature in asthma," emphasizes Albert L. Sheffer, M.D., of Harvard Medical School, the chairman of the Expert Panel. The experts now believe that airway inflammation is one of the primary mechanisms causing an asthmatic's airways to become hyperreactive.

Unlike some other lung diseases, such as emphysema, in asthma there is nothing wrong with the alveoli, the air sacs, themselves. The leaves of the tree are normal. Asthma is a disease of the air *tubes,* the branches of the tree.

Also in contrast to some other lung diseases, asthma attacks are, by definition, generally reversible. The attacks may subside by themselves with time, or the constricted bronchial tubes can be relaxed by treatment with various types of medications (see pages 111–19). And in between acute episodes, a child who has asthma usually looks and feels perfectly normal—although his or her airways still remain more hyperreactive than those of a child with normal lungs.

When a child does have an acute attack and his airways become constricted, he must work harder to breathe—the word "asthma" comes from the Greek word for panting—and he usually begins to wheeze, that is, make sounds as he breathes in and out. Doctors can detect this wheezing sound with their stethoscopes, but it sometimes is loud enough that a parent can hear it.

"If you put your ear to her chest," says one mother, "it sort of whistles as she breathes in and out. You can tell that her lungs are doing it, not her windpipe." Another mother adds, "With my kids, it is more like a rattle. You can hear that the air is not flowing freely, that there is a blockage there."

"These sounds," explains Dr. Pawlowski, "are made when the air encounters resistance to flow as the child breathes. Other, more coarse sounds are made when mucus is suddenly dislodged during breathing. When the airways become very narrow or very plugged with mucus, the child's chest becomes very quiet because so little air is able to flow. This is even more ominous than a noisy chest, in which some air movement is still occurring."

Some children with asthma cough instead of wheezing. Doctors call this "cough-variant asthma." These children cough "when the airways in just the upper part of their lungs are reacting," Dr. Pawlowski explains. "The mechanism causing this is unknown but probably involves reflex responses to irritation or inflammation."

And many asthmatic children both cough *and* wheeze. "In these children, the lower airways produce tremendous quantities of mucus. Clearance of this mucus is a major contributor to their coughing."

To the children themselves, "It's difficult to breathe. And it *feels* like there's an obstruction," says thirteen-year-old Mary Ann, "like the air has to go around something and is weaving in and out through your lungs. And I feel sort of light-headed. And the wheezing does make very strange sounds. You breathe one way, and it is like a little voice, and you breathe another way, and there is a different little voice."

When Michael has an attack, he says, he feels "real tight" and starts "getting pains in my chest. Walking a block, walking up stairs, any excess effort takes a lot out of you."

Many children wheeze and have their attacks more at night. "An increase in the lung's 'twitchiness' during late night to early morning hours is a relatively constant feature of asthma," notes Dr. Pawlowski. When Patrick was three years old, "he would be fine all day," explains his mother, "and then about four or five hours after he went to bed, he would wake up gasping and struggling for air. It was scary because it was the middle of the night. Just the darkness of the night made it so much more frightening."

In a severe attack, a child may start turning blue because he has less oxygen in the blood or even go into respiratory failure; that is, the child's respiratory system may not be able to provide enough oxygen for his body tissues. One woman recalls, "With the lack of oxygen, you stagger and slur your words and behave totally irrationally. It really does look like you have been drinking. And the terror. Am I going to die?"

Asthma varies enormously in the frequency, the severity and the suddenness of such attacks. Some people suffer only a few episodes throughout their entire lives: one woman has had just two attacks, one when she was a baby and a second that put her in the hospital when she was forty-five. Other asthmatics are constantly wheezing and are in and out of their doctor's offices all the time.

A child's asthma is considered moderate, says the Expert Panel Report, if he or she has episodes of wheezing or coughing more than once or twice a week (often at night) and misses some school. Children with severe asthma are those who wheeze and cough almost daily, whose sleep is interrupted almost every night, and whose school attendance is poor.

"Some children get attacks very, very suddenly; within hours, they are very sick," explains John R. Forehand, M.D., of The Children's Hospital of Philadelphia. "Other children take days to reach their peak of severity. The problem with asthma is that it is unpredictable. Children go back and forth between degrees of severity. They'll have a particularly bad year, and then they'll change. Or they may be mild all their life and then, all of a sudden, bingo, they'll get a big one."

"Some children have mild to moderate wheezing much of the time," adds Dr. Pawlowski. "These children can become so accustomed to this mild degree of 'air hunger' that when their wheezing does get worse, it can be quite difficult for them to appreciate the change in their condition. And children with moderate or severe asthma may also continue to have mild bronchoconstriction and airway plugging between their acute attacks—but not perceive it. The child could actually be short of breath and not realize it. He does not perceive breathlessness the same way as a child without asthma does."

Asthma can start at any age, but the disease most often first appears in childhood, sometimes even during the first few months of life. More than 50 percent of cases, says the Heart, Lung Institute's Expert Panel Report on asthma, begin during the first two years of life. David, for instance, was ten months old when he had his first attack. And in one morning recently at The Children's Hospital of Philadelphia, "we also saw two other infants," says allergist Lillian P. Kravis, M.D., "one only three months old and the other six months old, who both had asthma. This belies the common idea that asthma does not appear before the age of a year." Mary Ann was seven years old when her asthma "really appeared out of the blue," says her mother. Mary Ann had gone to stay overnight with a friend, "and then we got a phone call saying she wasn't feeling very well and couldn't breathe."

THE TRIGGERS OF ASTHMA

If your child has asthma, there are a variety of stimuli or triggers that may be precipitating his or her acute attacks and episodes of wheezing. "Every child is different," notes Dr. Pawlowski. "Each asthmatic reacts to a different set or combination of triggers."

Infections In babies and very young children—whose lungs are less developed and whose airways are smaller and more easily blocked—the triggers are usually viral respiratory tract infections. David's first attack, when he was ten months old, came when he caught a cold. David then continued to have "a very rough winter," recalls his mother. "He had many colds, and each time, he began wheezing." Adds Dr. Kravis, "We hear this story over and over again."

And after such a virus infection, "a child's airways may remain extra twitchy for variable periods of time," explains Dr. Pawlowski, "so that other triggers that the child normally tolerates well may bring on more wheezing."

Allergies to Airborne Substances In older children, among the common triggers are allergic reactions to substances in the air that they breathe. The same roster of airborne allergens that can cause the nose to run—*pollens* of trees, grasses and weeds; indoor and outdoor *molds; house-dust mites, cockroaches* and *other components of house dust;* and *dander* and other emanations from cats, dogs and various other animals (see Chapter 4, pages 61–66)—can also make their way down into the lungs and cause the bronchial muscles to contract. Some 75 to 85 percent of asthmatics, says the Expert Panel Report, have positive skin tests to these common, inhaled allergens. And many, many children who have asthma also suffer from allergic rhinitis. That is, they have runny noses as well as hyperreactive lungs.

With Mary Ann, the allergic triggers are cats and the fall-pollinating weeds. Her first attack, when she stayed with a friend overnight, came in September, when ragweed and other weeds are pollinating; her friend lived in the country and also had several cats. With Michael, it's cockroaches plus tree, grass and weed pollens. With Patrick, now seven, the triggers are primarily molds and animals. He tends to start wheezing when he plays outside on windy days, when outdoor mold counts can be high, or when one of his classmates comes to school with cat or dog hairs on him.

In the central valley of northern California, during May when grasses are pollinating, there are annual epidemics of asthma, when allergic people—many of whom never wheeze the rest of the year—flock to hospitals in great numbers. And in Barcelona, Spain, when ships in the harbor are unloading soybeans, the airborne dust triggers epidemics of allergic asthma that, over the past ten years, have sent hundreds of people to hospitals and caused at least twenty deaths.

"In many temperate areas, early fall is a particularly difficult time for asthmatics," points out Dr. Pawlowski, "and hospital admissions increase drastically. This is probably related to a combination of factors: a resurgence of respiratory viruses propagated during the return to school, children's laxity in taking their asthma medications during a relatively symptom-free summer and the heavy doses of pollens, especially ragweed, in August and September."

Allergies to Foods   Less commonly, children can have acute asthma attacks triggered by allergies to food. George, you recall from Chapter 2, page 25, wheezes if he eats any food containing wheat. It is very rare, however, that a food allergy causes asthma alone; it usually causes other symptoms as well. Whenever Bobby, whom we met in Chapter 1, page 7 and again in Chapter 2, pages 15–16, eats peanut butter or anything containing peanut oil, he not only starts to have trouble breathing and coughs a lot but he also throws up, his head and upper arms itch and his face swells.

Exercise   In some 70 to 80 percent of asthmatic children, simply exercising can trigger their attacks. This is called exercise-induced asthma, sometimes abbreviated "EIA"; doctors also sometimes call it "EIB," for exercise-induced bronchospasm. Peter, a thirteen-year-old sportsman who plays on lacrosse, soccer *and* ice hockey teams, finds—when he forgets to take his medicine—that when "you start running, you can't breathe and you have to stop playing. You have to come off and sit for a while."

And Olympic swimmer Nancy Hogshead, who won three gold medals and a silver in the 1984 Games in Los Angeles and who also has written a book called *Asthma & Exercise* (with co-author Gerald S. Couzens), tells that when she was a teenager she would repeatedly pass out after swimming practice or a race before she discovered that she suffers from exercise-induced asthma.

Other Triggers   Some asthmatics—about 2 to 4 percent, most of them adults—get asthma attacks if they take *aspirin.* Others are set off when they ingest *sulfites,* preservatives that are widely added to many foods, including dried fruits, maraschino cherries, beer and wine and also to some medications. Wines, prescription drugs and all packaged foods now must be labeled if they contain sulfites, and in 1986, the Food and Drug Administration prohibited the use of sulfites on fruit and other produce in salad bars. In 1990, the agency extended this ban to fresh, peeled potatoes, after the agency had received nearly one thousand complaints of adverse reactions, including four deaths, from sulfite-treated potatoes in restaurants. Up to a million asthmatics, says the FDA, may be sensitive to sulfites.

As with allergic rhinitis, children with asthmatic lungs may also become hypersensitive to various *irritating substances* such as *tobacco smoke, perfumes, paint fumes, cooking odors and other smells* and *soap powders* and *various dusts.* One asthmatic woman won a seventy-five-thousand-dollar settlement from a New York department store after a demonstrator sprayed her with perfume and she suffered an attack that sent her to the hospital for ten days. Several components of *air pollution—sulfur dioxide, nitrogen oxides, ozone*—can also trigger acute attacks in some asthmatics.

"So-called *'passive smoking'* is a common problem for children who have asthma," emphasizes Dr. Pawlowski. "It has been well documented that asthmatic children who are chronically exposed to tobacco smoke have considerably more difficulty with their asthma. While exposure to smoke may not always trigger an acute attack by itself, it can add to the baseline twitchiness of your child's airways and thus make his or her response to other triggers much worse." See Chapter 9, pages 158–59, for more about the effect of second-hand tobacco smoke on children.

Changes in the weather bother some people with asthma. *Cold air* can be a trigger. One downhill skier starts to wheeze whenever she comes directly indoors on very cold days; she has learned to eat lunch outdoors and at the end of the day to come inside gradually, pausing for a while in the foyer or mudroom. And seven-year-old Patrick sometimes has an attack when he gets the *giggles,* "whooping and hollering," as his mother puts it.

And some people suffer asthma attacks without any obvious triggers. Physicians call this *"intrinsic" asthma.*

What Causes Asthma?

Children who develop asthma have inherited a *genetic predisposition* toward the disease, and asthma tends to run in families. Judy, for example, has allergic asthma—and so does her father and one of her brothers. People with asthma are also likely to have close relatives who have eczema or allergic rhinitis. Michael's mother and younger brother both have allergic rhinitis. And one asthmatic man has a daughter and a granddaughter with allergic rhinitis and another granddaughter who has eczema. Among identical twins (who by definition have identical genes), when one twin has asthma, the second one also has the disease 15 to 20 percent of the time, about twice as often as among fraternal twins (who do not share the same genes).

It is clear, however, that more than just heredity is involved. The fact that identical twins do *not* both have the disease 80 to 85 percent of the time is evidence of significant *environmental factors*. Researchers believe that these may include such things as infections or exposure to various airborne allergens. While some components of air pollution trigger attacks in some asthmatics, it is not known whether air pollution can actually cause asthma to develop in the first place.

There are still many mysteries about asthma. In children under ten, boys develop the disease twice as often as girls, but girls catch up later in life. And there are wild—and unexplained—variations in the prevalence of asthma from country to country. Both Australia and New Zealand have twice as much asthma, proportionally, as the United States. And some groups of peoples—among them, American Indians, Eskimos, Tibetans and West Africans—very rarely suffer from asthma.

Nor do scientists fully understand all the physiological mechanisms involved in asthma. As with other allergies (see Chapter 1, pages 11–13), children with allergic asthma have IgE antibodies against the specific substances to which they are allergic. Mary Ann, who is allergic to cats and ragweed pollen, has anti-cat and anti-ragweed-pollen IgE antibodies. Michael, who is allergic to cockroaches, among other things, has anti-cockroach IgE antibodies.

When Michael inhales cockroach allergens, the molecules make their way down into his lungs and there combine with the antibodies, which are attached to mast cells and other inflammatory, immune-system cells in the mucous membranes lining his lungs. This causes the mast cells to burst and release histamine and the other biochemical substances, the mediators, which produce his allergic symptoms.

Yet this is only part of the story. Not all asthma, you will recall, *is* allergic. In exercise-induced asthma, physicians believe that the loss of heat or water, or both, in the airways of the lungs—due to breathing in air that is cooler and drier than that of the lungs—causes the mast cells to release their inflammatory mediators.

These biochemical mediators "initiate a chain reaction of events," explains Harvard's Dr. Sheffer. The mediators cause the asthmatic person's bronchial muscles to contract; the mucous membranes to swell, become inflamed and secrete more mucus; and more and more inflammatory cells to flock into the airways. These changes make the person's airways more hyperresponsive, more obstructed and—by damaging the tissues lining the airways—even more sensitive to airborne allergens and irritants.

"This inflammatory component of asthma, which is more irreversible than the bronchospasm, is the component of asthma that we are just now learning about," notes Dr. Forehand. "Inflammation is one of the hot areas in asthma research right now."

DIAGNOSING ASTHMA

There are a number of other diseases and conditions that can mimic asthma and also cause your child to wheeze or make other abnormal sounds as he breathes. Among them are *infectious diseases* such as pneumonia, bronchitis and bronchiolitis and also *cystic fibrosis* (one of the most common genetic diseases). Or your child may get something—a piece of food, a small toy or some other *foreign object*—lodged in his throat, windpipe or the airways of his lungs. Or a child may have been born with any of a number of *congenital abnormalities* of the respiratory, gastrointestinal or cardiovascular systems that can create obstructions to airflow in the respiratory tree. And some children may wheeze because of lingering *bronchopulmonary dysplasia,* the lung disease associated with premature birth. "In these children," explains Dr. Pawlowski, "the hyperreactivity of their airways is closely linked with the scarring that they have in their lungs."

However, recurrent episodes of coughing and wheezing,

in both children and adults, says the Expert Panel Report, are almost always due to asthma. Underdiagnosis of asthma occurs most often, says the report, "when young children who wheeze only when they have respiratory infections are dismissed as having wheezy bronchitis, asthmatic bronchitis, bronchitis or pneumonia."

Pulmonary-Function Tests   The most important tests for diagnosing whether or not your child has asthma—and also for assessing its severity—are what physicians call "pulmonary-function tests," which they often abbreviate "PFT's." These tests make objective measurements of how well your child's lungs are working. The physicians often use an instrument known as a *spirometer*. "Spiro-" comes from the Latin word for breath, and "-meter" means measure. A spirometer thus measures a person's breathing. All patients suspected of having asthma, stresses the Expert Panel Report, should have spirometry performed. "Pulmonary function studies," stresses the report, "are essential for diagnosing asthma."

In the Allergy Clinic at The Children's Hospital of Philadelphia, the spirometer that they use these days is a computerized "birthday cake machine." A picture of a birthday cake with twelve candles appears on the computer screen, and the child blows into a mouthpiece. "Take a real deep breath," Shea Rosen, R.N., the allergy nurse, coaches the children. "Then blow it out all at once. Try to blow out as many candles as you can." The computer automatically measures the volume of air that the child blows out and also how fast he can blow it out. Then the machine draws a graph of the child's breath and calculates his score.

If the child's scores are below normal for his age and size, the physicians may have him inhale a dose of a medication that can quickly open up constricted airways. Then they have him repeat the pulmonary-function tests. Since asthma, by definition, is a reversible obstruction of the airways, if the child does get a higher score the second time around, it is evidence that he does have asthma rather than some other lung disease.

Sometimes, the physicians at The Children's Hospital may have children with more severe asthma undergo more sophisticated lung tests in the hospital's Pulmonary Function Laboratory. There the child sits inside an instrumented compartment about the size and shape of a telephone booth. The child blows into a mouthpiece, and a computer measures still other aspects of his or her breathing, such as the air pressure in the lungs, the resistance in the lungs to the flow of air and the total volume of air the lungs can hold, including the amount that one cannot blow out, and that remains in the lungs between breaths. Children who have poorly controlled asthma usually have lung volumes larger than normal; their lungs are hyperinflated due to air trapped behind their obstructed, small airways.

If the physicians suspect that a child may have exercise-induced asthma, they can have him walk briskly on a treadmill in the Pulmonary Function Laboratory, while instruments monitor his heart rate and the amount of oxygen in his blood. Then they measure the child's breathing again to discover whether the exercise caused the flow of air in his lungs to decrease.

Skin Tests   To find out whether allergies are contributing to a child's wheezing, as they do in so many asthmatic children, allergists may order skin tests, which detect whether the child has IgE antibodies against various specific allergenic substances. See Chapter 8, pages 125–28, for an explanation of how skin tests are performed, what they show and their limitations and risks.

Bronchial Challenges   Occasionally the physicians will have a child undergo what they call a "bronchial challenge." They have the child inhale a substance (usually histamine or methacholine) that causes the muscles surrounding the bronchial tubes to contract, and they measure the child's lung functions before and after this challenge. Children who have asthma react to much lower doses of these chemicals than do children with normal lungs.

If your child turns out to have moderate or severe asthma, the Heart, Lung Institute's Expert Panel Report on asthma recommends that he or she be evaluated by a physician who specializes in the diagnosing and treatment of asthma—usually an allergist or a pulmonologist (an expert in lung diseases).

TREATING ASTHMA

Prevention of acute asthma attacks, stresses the Expert Panel Report, is an important principle of treatment for asthma.

Avoiding Triggers The primary way of preventing a child's asthma attacks is for him to avoid, if possible, whatever circumstances or substances, ingested or inhaled, trigger his episodes. "Each patient must learn to understand his or her own set of triggers," emphasizes Dr. Pawlowski, "so that he or she can learn how to avoid them when possible."

The majority of asthmatic children whose attacks are triggered by *allergies* should try to avoid the allergens—foods, pollens, mites, cockroaches, molds, animal emanations—that are provoking their symptoms. For a discussion of avoiding allergenic foods, see Chapter 2, pages 29–32. For a discussion of how you can help your child avoid airborne allergens, see Chapter 9, pages 151–58.

Allergy Shots Many children whose asthma is triggered by inhaled allergens can be helped by a course of immunotherapy (that is, allergy shots) for the specific substances to which they are allergic. See Chapter 8, pages 141–45, for detailed information about allergy shots, how allergists give them, how they work and their possible side effects.

Medications There is now an arsenal of anti-asthma medications that can control symptoms and prevent acute attacks in the overwhelming majority of children with asthma.

BRONCHODILATORS: THEOPHYLLINE Among the most important of these anti-asthma drugs is a category called the bronchodilators. These are medications that relax tight bronchial muscles and thus dilate—that is, open up—constricted airways in the lungs and allow your child to breathe more easily and stop wheezing. There are two types of bronchodilators that physicians commonly prescribe for children. One is theophylline, which children take by mouth, either as a liquid, capsules, tablets or in the form of fine sprinkles that parents can mix with a child's food. "It is also available in a form for rectal administration," adds Dr. Kravis, "for children who are vomiting early on at the start of an attack."

ADRENALINE-LIKE DRUGS The other type of bronchodilators that doctors prescribe for children are the so-called *beta-adrenergic agonists,* a group of drugs related chemically to adrenaline, one of the natural hormones produced by our adrenal glands. One of the beta-adrenergics is ephinephrine, which, you recall from previous chapters, physicians may inject for emergency treatment of severe allergic reactions to foods, stinging-insect venoms and drugs. Doctors also sometimes inject epinephrine to treat acute attacks of asthma; epinephrine shots for asthma, however, are currently giving way to the use of other adrenaline-like drugs such as albuterol, metaproterenol, isoproterenol and terbutaline. "These drugs are tailor-made to mimic adrenaline's effects on the airways more selectively," explains Dr. Pawlowski, "and they thus have few side effects."

Children take some of these other beta-adrenergic drugs by mouth, but frequently they inhale them from devices called *"metered-dose inhalers"* (often abbreviated "MDI's"), small aerosol canisters that deliver a measured dose of the drug.

Sometimes children spray the drug directly into their mouth and then inhale it into their lungs. Other times, children may inhale these drugs with the help of a baglike device called a *spacer*. First they spray the drug from the MDI into the spacer. Next they draw the drug into their mouth from the spacer, and then they inhale the drug into their lungs. The spacer "helps children coordinate the timing of the spray," explains Dr. Pawlowski, "with the slow, deep, prolonged inspiration of the drug."

Instead of using a metered-dose inhaler, with or without a spacer, some children inhale beta-adrenergic medications from a *nebulizer*. This is an electrical machine about the size of a double-toaster, with an air compressor inside. A parent pours liquid medication into a small plastic cup, and the machine turns it into a fine mist. A baby can inhale the drugs from a mask; older children use a mouthpiece. "The child has to sit down and relax for about ten minutes and take multiple breaths," says Dr. Sharon K. Sweinberg of The Children's Hospital of Philadelphia. "Initially, the nebulizer treatment opens the airways that are farther up in the lungs, and then the longer the child uses the nebulizer, the more the medications penetrate to the periphery of the lungs." Adds Dr. Pawlowski, "These nebulizers are particularly useful for children under the age of five."

"Inhaled therapy is superior to oral therapy," stresses the Heart, Lung Institute's Expert Panel Report on asthma, because inhaled medications work faster, involve lower dosages and cause fewer side effects.

Some children take these adrenaline-like drugs regularly, every day, to prevent attacks, but these medications also relax bronchial muscles and dilate airways quickly enough that they can help alleviate an attack in progress. "If you are wheezing and you inhale albuterol," says Roger Danziger, M.D., of The Children's Hospital of Philadelphia, "everything opens up and you feel better."

ANTI-INFLAMMATORY DRUGS In the past, these bronchodilating medications—theophylline and the adrenaline-like drugs—have been the mainstay of drug treatment for asthma. Now, with the new appreciation of the role of inflammation, the experts are recommending that many asthmatics also take anti-inflammatory medication. "Reducing and hopefully preventing inflammation, not just reversing bronchial constriction, is central to asthma management," says Harvard's Dr. Sheffer. "This means not only using a bronchodilator to provide immediate symptomatic relief, but also using anti-inflammatory agents to reduce inflammation over the long term."

CROMOLYN One of the anti-inflammatory drugs that physicians commonly prescribe for children who have asthma is cromolyn. Children with allergic rhinitis, you recall, spray cromolyn into their nose. (See Chapter 4, page 76.) Similarly, children with asthma spray cromolyn into their mouth, from a metered-dose inhaler, with or without a spacer, and then inhale it into their lungs. Or, as with the adrenaline-like medications, they may inhale the cromolyn from a nebulizer.

Cromolyn is strictly a preventive medication; it does not help relieve asthma attacks in progress. "If you were having an acute asthma attack and took a cromolyn inhaler," Dr. Pawlowski explains, "it wouldn't do anything. But if you have been inhaling cromolyn for a couple of weeks, regularly, your system has a base level of the drug that would dampen your allergy-triggered asthma symptoms. Cromolyn also has the effect of minimizing the amounts of other medications that you need to take."

CORTICOSTEROIDS The other category of anti-inflammatory medication that asthmatic children take are the corticosteroids. "Corticosteroids are the most effective anti-inflammatory drugs," says the Expert Panel Report. In contrast to cromolyn, corticosteroids can act both to prevent the triggering of airway inflammation *and* to reduce the severity of ongoing inflammation, thus helping to open up a child's airways.

Children with severe asthma may need to take corticosteroids by mouth. When taken orally for long periods of time, corticosteroids can produce serious side effects (see pages 138–40). "Generally, we use just short bursts of oral steroids," says Dr. Kravis. However, a relatively small number of children who have asthma become "steroid-dependent"; that is, they must take corticosteroids by mouth more or less continually to keep their asthma under control and to prevent acute attacks.

Much more commonly, children take corticosteroids by inhaling them from a metered-dose inhaler, with or without a spacer. Corticosteroids cause far fewer side effects when they are inhaled. "Inhaled corticosteroids are safe and effective for the treatment of asthma," emphasizes the Expert Panel Report. "The use of inhaled corticosteroids reduces the need for the chronic use of oral steroids. Inhaled corticosteroids are being used more frequently as primary therapy for moderate and severe asthma."

"People are often very scared of steroids," adds Dr. Kravis. "It is important that parents understand that if the child inhales the corticosteroids in proper doses there is nothing to be afraid of."

Because of this new understanding of the role of inflammation in asthma, pharmacological researchers are currently working to develop additional categories of anti-inflammatory medications for asthma, drugs that would block the physiological mechanisms that produce the inflammation.

ANTIHISTAMINES The antihistamines, which are so useful for treating so many kinds of allergies, probably do not help asthma at all. Physicians may, however, prescribe antihistamines to control nose or skin symptoms in the many asthmatic children who also have other allergic disorders. "The classic antihistamines offer virtually no relief for the asthmatic lung," notes Dr. Pawlowski, "but there are newer formulations now being developed that may be more efficacious for asthma."

See Chapter 8, pages 129–41, for more detailed information about all of these drugs, how they are used, what they accomplish, what is known about how they work and their possible side effects.

How Children Take These Medications   "There is no one way to treat asthma," points out Dr. Pawlowski. Different children take different amounts and different combinations of these anti-asthma medications, depending on their age, what their triggers are and also the severity of their disease. Children's specific drug regimens usually also change over time, as their symptoms may wax and wane.

And when your child first begins a regimen of anti-asthma medications, it may take him or her "a couple of weeks to get up to snuff with all the medications," says Dr. Pawlowski, that is, for the drugs to become fully effective and also for you and your child to learn how to administer them successfully.

Because it is important to detect an impending asthma attack early in its course (see Chapter 9, pages 163–65), some children monitor their own breathing at home, using a device called a *peak-flow meter*. This is a simple, portable device several inches long and an inch or two in diameter. Your child takes a deep breath and blows, as hard as he can, into a mouthpiece at one end, and the peak-flow meter automatically measures and displays the number of liters of air your child can force out of his lungs in one minute. The Expert Panel Report recommends that physicians consider having children five years and older who have moderate to severe asthma use peak-flow meters at home.

Some children use a peak-flow meter every morning and evening, and their parents have specific, standing instructions from their physician to increase medications if the child's peak-flow falls below a certain number. The use of a peak-flow meter can help spot an oncoming asthma attack before you or your child are otherwise aware that the child is in trouble. "Regular peak-flow measurements," emphasizes the Expert Panel Report, "can help detect early signs of asthma episodes before symptoms occur."

Peak-flow meters are particularly useful, points out Dr. Pawlowski, for those children who have mild to moderate wheezing much of the time and become so accustomed to wheezing that they have trouble recognizing when it gets worse. "This is quite serious if your child cannot report that he is worse," emphasizes Dr. Pawlowski. "Home monitoring with a peak-flow meter, combined with frequent checkups by the physician, will lead to a better understanding of the severity of your child's illness. Your child will receive better treatment and be much less likely to suffer a severe episode.

"A peak-flow meter can also assist in tracking down specific triggers in your child's environment that are causing trouble," continues Dr. Pawlowski. "Upon exposure to the trigger, his or her peak-flow readings would decrease."

Since asthma is a chronic disease, it "requires *continuous medical care,*" the Expert Panel Report stresses, "to control symptoms and prevent acute exacerbations." Children must return periodically to their physicians for checkups, sometimes every month. Children also need to repeat their lung-function tests at intervals to find out how well they are responding to treatment and whether the doses of their medications need to be adjusted. With theophylline, there is a fairly narrow range between too high a dose, which could be toxic (see Chapter 8, pages 134–35), and too low a dose; children who are taking theophylline need to have their blood levels of the drug measured regularly to make sure they are getting the right amount.

For children with mild, intermittent asthma, the medication of choice, says the Expert Panel Report, is one of the beta-adrenergics. Many children have asthma so mild, explains Dr. Forehand, that they "require only this one drug and that only from time to time when they need it. These children are fine most of the time. Occasionally they may cough or have chest discomfort, but if they inhale a beta-adrenergic bronchodilator, they will be fine. The child just needs a puff, and that's it. When parents are told that their child has asthma, that may very well be the scenario."

Other children, with more severe asthma, must take one or two or more medications regularly, every day. Many patients need round-the-clock medication, says the Expert Panel Report. Children who have poor exercise tolerance, recurring symptoms and frequent symptoms at night "will often benefit," says the report, "from the regular administration and more aggressive use of anti-asthma medication, especially anti-inflammatory medicine."

Fourteen-month-old David, for instance, the young fellow who begins wheezing every time he gets a cold, takes albuterol and cromolyn twice a day, in the morning and evening, by means of a nebulizer. When he does get a cold and starts to have trouble, his mother—at his doctor's instructions —increases David's nebulizer treatments to four times a day and also adds liquid albuterol three times a day. "He loves it. It tastes like apricots," says David's mother. This regimen "usually takes care of it."

Thirteen-year-old Mary Ann, who has allergic asthma, takes theophylline, by mouth, twice a day, and from time to time, if she starts to wheeze or is going to visit a friend who has a cat, she also takes albuterol and an antihistamine. Before Mary Ann's physician put her on this maintenance dosage, she had had several bad attacks that required emergency treatment. Since she has been on these medications, says her mother, "we really haven't had any problem. Everything is under good control."

Some 90 percent of people with exercise-induced asthma can prevent attacks just by inhaling albuterol or cromolyn before gym class or other exercise. For Olympic swimmer Nancy Hogshead, "controlling my asthma now is a relatively simple matter," she explains in *Asthma & Exercise*. "Twenty minutes before I go to exercise, I take my two puffs from an albuterol inhaler and then I'm out the door."

Others with exercise-induced asthma need more than one drug. Peter, the thirteen-year-old who plays soccer, lacrosse *and* ice hockey, takes theophylline twice a day and also "five minutes before a game." He explains, "You take two puffs, from the 'whiffer,' " as he calls his albuterol inhaler. "I'm real forgetful," he confesses. "I can never remember to take it." But when he starts playing, he remembers in a hurry when "you find you can't breathe."

Thirteen-year-old Judy, who has severe allergic asthma and also allergic rhinitis, now takes three anti-asthma medications, theophylline, albuterol and cromolyn, and also an antihistamine for her runny nose. Before this regimen, "we went through about five years of hell," says her mother. "Our lives, everything, revolved around the asthma. She was constantly having attacks. I lived in the doctor's office. She was on and off oral corticosteroids constantly. At one point when she was on them for five weeks, she gained almost fifteen pounds. It was horrible. I had this little girl who completely changed in physical appearance." Then the doctors at the hospital, "I think, finally put her on the right amount of medicine," and Judy also started taking allergy shots. "In the last two years, she has only been on steroids once for five days. Her nose is less runny, and she has reduced her dose of antihistamines. She's doing wonderfully. Now the asthma is just a nuisance. It really doesn't stop her from doing anything."

Treating Asthma Emergencies   Fifteen to twenty children each day, most days, arrive in The Children's Hospital of Philadelphia's Emergency Department in the throes of an acute asthma attack. "They probably make up 10 percent of all our patients," says Dr. Steven M. Selbst, Director of the

Emergency Department. "We see them all year long, winter and summer, but fall is the worst time. And it occurs in clusters. Some days there seems to be something out there. It probably has something to do with the weather; damp or rainy days are bad asthma days. Most of the children are in pretty significant respiratory distress. They are breathing very fast, and their chests are moving in and out. And a few are very severe; they are blue and really gasping and struggling."

As soon as possible, a respiratory therapist starts giving the children aerosol treatments, every twenty minutes or half-hour, with a bronchodilating drug, usually albuterol or metaproterenol. "In some cases," continues Dr. Selbst, "we give shots of epinephrine. That's what we used to do all the time, but in recent years, we've found that the aerosols work just as well, maybe better, and they are certainly better tolerated by children. No child wants to get shots." Most children also get oxygen, and if, after two or three aerosol treatments, they are not responding, the physicians may start giving them theophylline intravenously.

If the child still does not respond, the physicians admit him or her to the hospital, where they can continue to give intravenous theophylline and also intravenous corticosteroid, and the respiratory therapists can keep giving the child frequent aerosol treatments. Most children recover enough to be discharged in three or four days.

A very small percentage of asthmatic children have attacks so severe that they must go to the Intensive Care Unit, where they can receive an even more potent bronchodilator, isoproterenol, intravenously or by inhalation. Since isoproterenol can affect the heart, these children must be monitored constantly while receiving it. In extremely severe cases of respiratory failure, a child may need to be on a respirator temporarily, to take over the work of breathing and supply sufficient oxygen to his body tissues.

* * *

One young man who has been admitted to The Children's Hospital of Philadelphia more times than he can remember and has also done time in the Intensive Care Unit is Michael, who has had severe allergic asthma "all my life. I guess it was first diagnosed when I was two. I've had some real bad attacks," he explains. "They had me on steroids for years. In high school, in ninth and tenth grades, I had asthma so bad that by the time I walked up to the third floor, I had to stop and catch my breath; that would sometimes make me late to class. I was in the hospital, it seemed like every two months. I missed so much school, I had to go to summer school to make up Algebra I."

Michael's worst episode came two years ago. "I was doing pretty good. Every time I would have an attack, I would just sit home, maybe for a week, and take my treatment three or four times a day. But that day I was taking it every two hours and it didn't work." When Michael finally went to the hospital, he ended up on a respirator in the Intensive Care Unit for ten days. "They didn't think I was going to pull through. I guess I really scared a lot of people."

Today, Michael has just turned twenty and is a college sophomore who also works part time. He takes theophylline and also inhales albuterol and cromolyn, from a nebulizer, twice a day. "Before I go work out and lift weights with my friends at school, I take my spray, my albuterol inhaler," and when he gets a cold, he usually must take a burst of corticosteroid, "about three times a winter." He has not had to be admitted to the hospital or visit the emergency room since his big attack. To the casual eye, Michael today looks perfectly normal. "The asthma's gotten better," he says. "I can run up stairs now. Hopefully, it will continue."

"Fortunately, not many people with asthma have the disease as severely as Michael," says Dr. Sweinberg. "We can count on one hand the number of children who come here to Children's Hospital who are that severe."

* * *

The fact that asthma can, on occasion, kill was brought to popular attention recently when the chancellor of the New York City school system dropped dead of an asthma attack at the age of fifty-two. However, asthma is a relatively rare cause of death. It kills about 4,000 to 5,000 Americans each year, the great majority of them older adults. In 1988 (the most recent year for which figures are available), asthma killed 119 children under the age of fifteen.

To put this figure in perspective, 22,000 children die each year of injuries, which is the number-one killer of children, according to the Public Health Service's Center for Disease Control. More than 10,000 children a year are killed in automobile accidents. Nearly 3,000 are murdered. More than 2,000 commit suicide; some 2,000 drown and about 1,500 die of burns.

Nevertheless, physicians are very concerned about asthma deaths among children because they believe that most of them are preventable and because their numbers have been rising. In 1979, asthma killed 63 children under fifteen, only about half the number as in 1988. And the death rate among young, nonwhite males is nearly five times the rate among whites.

The reasons for the increase are not clear. "The thing that is very upsetting," says Dr. Kravis, "is that we have all these advances in therapeutic agents, and there is a greater recognition of the fact that asthma can be a serious problem." Hospitalizations for asthma are increasing, "indicating that parents know that a child is sick enough to be hospitalized. You'd expect the deaths to be down, but the change in fatalities has been up. And that's difficult to explain." Too high doses of some of the anti-asthma drugs could conceivably explain some deaths, but physicians believe that many more deaths are due to undermedication than overmedication. "Most deaths are related to undertreatment," concludes the Expert Panel Report. Less than half the deaths occur in hospitals. "And there are some patients who just die suddenly," adds Dr. Kravis. "They seem to be in their usual state of health, and then they just keel over."

Furthermore, the prevalence of asthma also seems to be rising. Some of the increase may be due to the fact that physicians are now diagnosing asthma more accurately, thanks to the recent availability of computerized pulmonary-function testing. Much of what doctors used to call bronchitis, they now recognize is asthma. However, there are many other possible factors. Some physicians believe that increased exposure to house-dust mites and other indoor allergens, thanks to our modern, relatively airtight houses, may be a factor.

"It is not entirely clear whether the incidence of asthma has actually been increasing," says Dr. Kravis, "or whether its severity is increasing, or whether the recognition of asthma is becoming more widespread and therefore more patients are sent to the hospital. There are very perplexing aspects to this illness, which we do not entirely understand."

WHAT HAPPENS AS A CHILD GROWS

Fortunately, "most children who have asthma tend to improve greatly around adolescence," Dr. Kravis continues. Patrick's mother, for one, had asthma as a child. She developed the disease when she was about seven years old, but "it was largely gone," she says, by the time she was fourteen.

Other people, however, can develop asthma for the first time even when they are adults. One woman had her first attack when she was in her late twenties and visited a friend who had fifteen cats. And one man, who has a daughter with allergic rhinitis, developed asthma when he was in his mid-sixties.

Nevertheless, the vast majority of children who have asthma grow up to lead long and productive lives. Theodore Roosevelt had severe asthma as a child, starting when he was about three years old, yet as an adult he not only became

President of the United States, from 1901 to 1909, but was a vigorous outdoorsman, soldier and champion of our national parks.

And many of our best Olympic athletes have asthma. In the 1984 Games in Los Angeles—swimmer Nancy Hogshead has tallied in her book *Asthma & Exercise*—sixty-seven of the American athletes had the disease and yet won a total of forty-one medals. Four years later, in the 1988 Games in Seoul, Korea, fifty-three of the competing Americans had asthma—and still won sixteen medals: five golds, ten silvers and one bronze.

CHAPTER 8

What Doctors Can Do About Allergies and Asthma

We have discussed diagnostic tests and treatments that physicians employ for just one type of allergic disorder— elimination diets for food allergy, for example, and lung-function tests for asthma—in the chapter on that particular disorder.

In this chapter, we will describe tests and treatments that apply to more than one allergic disorder: skin tests, the many medications used to treat allergies and asthma and immunotherapy (allergy shots). At the end of the chapter, we also discuss some unproven methods that parents may occasionally encounter.

SKIN TESTING

The most important, time-honored tests that physicians use for diagnosing allergies are skin tests. Skin tests are simple, relatively inexpensive and fast: within a half an hour or so, an allergist can find out whether or not a patient's body is capable of mounting an allergic response to each of perhaps dozens of different substances suspected of causing allergic symptoms.

Skin tests are available for a variety of foods; for many inhaled allergens, including pollens, molds, house-dust mites and animal danders; and for six stinging insects (honeybee, yellow jacket, yellow hornet, white-faced hornet, *Polistes* paper wasp and imported fire ant). Skin tests are available, however, for only a handful of drugs, and among antibiotics, only for penicillin.

The allergists at The Children's Hospital of Philadelphia skin test children only for substances that they have some reason to suspect may be causing a child's allergies. If a child has rhinitis primarily in the spring, say, when trees are pollinating, they test him for the pollens of the most common trees. If a child has year-round rhinitis or asthma and also a cat at home, they test him for cat dander. However, Children's Hospital allergists do not test a child for pollens unless he has seasonal symptoms or for an animal dander unless he is exposed to that animal. They consider it unethical to skin test a child for substances blindly—that is, without some grounds for suspicion.

The Allergy Clinic at Children's Hospital uses several different methods of performing skin tests. The one they employ most commonly is the *prick test.* For each allergen being tested, allergy nurse Shea Rosen, R.N., places a drop of a dilute extract of the substance on the child's skin. Then, with a special two-pronged needle, she quickly pricks through each drop into the upper layers of skin, to push the substance into the skin. The child usually lies on his stomach, and Mrs. Rosen places rows of extract drops—often many rows—on his back. Sometimes she places the drops on a child's arm instead.

"They all ask the same question," says Mrs. Rosen. " 'Is it going to hurt?' " The drops of extracts feel like drops of water, and most children say that the pricking part of the tests does not hurt. Most children do not even flinch.

The child must then lie still on his stomach or hold his arm quiet—for some, this is the hard part—so that the drops do not run together or roll off, for ten or fifteen minutes. If a child is allergic to a given substance, oak pollen, say, the skin under that drop develops, in effect, a hive, what allergists call a wheal-and-flare: a central bump (the wheal), surrounded by a larger, reddened area (the flare). To read a test, Mrs. Rosen simply measures the wheal and flare with a ruler.

In each battery of tests, allergists include both a negative and a positive control. The negative control is salt water; it should not cause a wheal-and-flare in anyone. The positive control is histamine itself, the best known of the biochemical substances, the mediators, that cause the allergic symptoms. Histamine should cause a wheal-and-flare on the skin of every child. While the pricking part of the testing does not hurt significantly, positive tests can itch. Mrs. Rosen rubs on corticosteroid cream to reduce the itching and occasionally gives a child antihistamines by mouth or even oral corticosteroid if a child has a large reaction.

For children too young to lie still long enough for these prick tests, Children's Hospital allergists use a small plastic device that can place drops of eight different extracts on the child's skin at once and also scratch through them all at the same time. The mother usually holds the child in her arms, and Mrs. Rosen simply presses the device against the child's back. This does hurt a little; most of the babies cry out momentarily.

Occasionally, if these skin tests are not conclusive, the allergists perform what they call *intradermal tests,* in which they inject drops of extracts into deeper, although still superficial, layers of the child's skin. Intradermal tests are more sensitive than the prick tests because the intradermals introduce greater amounts of the allergen into the skin.

What skin tests detect is whether or not a child has IgE antibodies in his skin against the specific allergens tested. If he does, the allergenic molecules in the extract combine with the antibody molecules on mast cells in his skin. This causes the mast cells to release histamine and the other biochemical substances, the mediators—producing the wheal-and-flare reaction. If your child is allergic to cats, say, the test will thus specifically detect anti-cat antibodies in his skin.

A limitation of skin testing, however, is that there is not an absolute, 100 percent correlation between skin test results and a child's symptoms. Your child can have a positive skin test to an allergenic substance and yet not show any symptoms when he or she is directly exposed to that substance. Such a positive test in the absence of symptoms, however, may indicate that a child is likely to develop an allergy to this substance at some time in the future.

The reverse situation can also be true: your child can be allergic to a substance yet still have a negative skin test to it. This may be true of skin tests for foods, in particular, which are not as reliable as those for inhaled allergens. For many foods, scientists have not yet identified the specific protein molecules responsible for allergic reactions. In some cases, the offending, allergenic molecules may not even exist in the intact food itself; they may instead be produced in the allergic person's gastrointestinal tract during the process of digestion.

And like all medical tests, skin tests have some risks. Because the tests expose a person to substances to which he or she may be allergic, there is a remote possibility that he or she may have a life-threatening anaphylactic reaction (see Chapter 2, pages 16–17). A recent survey of allergists located four deaths from skin testing over a ten-year period; all four followed intradermal (rather than prick) tests. While this number is probably an undercount, it is exceedingly small considering the many millions of skin tests that allergists perform every year. The most common side effect of skin tests is local itching, which may occasionally continue for hours. Nevertheless, whenever doctors administer skin tests, they are careful to observe people for any more significant reactions.

ANTI-ALLERGY AND ANTI-ASTHMA MEDICATIONS

Antihistamines   Antihistamines have been in use for nearly half a century, since the early 1940s, and today they are still one of the most widely used of all anti-allergy medications.

Children who suffer acute allergic reactions to foods, stinging-insect venoms or drugs or who have allergic skin disorders (eczema, hives, angioedema or contact dermatitis) take antihistamines by mouth to help reduce the itching and swelling.

Children who have allergic rhinitis take antihistamines regularly to reduce sneezing, itching and the runny discharge from their nose.

And while most antihistamines do nothing to help asthma itself, many children who have asthma take antihistamines because they also have allergic rhinitis. According to the authoritative 1991 Expert Panel Report on asthma from the National Heart, Lung and Blood Institute, "the long-held concern that antihistamines might worsen asthma as a result of a putative drying effect on bronchial mucus has not been verified."

Antihistamines usually start working quickly, within a half an hour or so of a person's taking them. As their name implies, the antihistamines work by blocking the action of histamine, the best known of the many biochemical substances, the mediators, released by mast cells during the allergic reaction. The antihistamines are able to block the action of histamine because they block the molecules (receptors) that it reacts with on its target cells.

The primary side effect of the antihistamines is that—in some people—they produce drowsiness and sedation. "For some reason, adults tend to be more sensitive than children to this effect," says allergist Sharon K. Sweinberg, M.D., of The Children's Hospital of Philadelphia. "They oftentimes will get very tired."

"The other possible problem with the antihistamines is that a child may have a bit of dizziness or light-headedness," explains Nicholas A. Pawlowski, M.D., Director of the Allergy Section at The Children's Hospital of Philadelphia. "Or in some children, antihistamines may stimulate them. But the major thing is the sleepiness. Beyond that, there is really not much to worry about with the antihistamines."

However, teenagers and adults should be aware that drinking alcohol intensifies this sedative effect of the antihistamines, and that they also should be careful about driving a car when they are taking them. "Most people who get very sleepy from antihistamines appreciate it," points out Dr. Pawlowski, "but it's an individual thing. A lot of people have no problem with them whatever. But anyone who is taking antihistamines for the first time should hold off driving until he or she really finds out what his or her own response is."

There are dozens of different antihistamines, however, some over-the-counter, some prescription, and they fall into six different chemical classes. If your child becomes too sedated or has other side effects from one type of antihistamine, your physician will probably suggest that he or she simply try another type. "Sometimes it is just a matter of switching antihistamine classes," says Dr. Pawlowski. Diphenhydramine, for instance, which is a very commonly used antihistamine, belongs to one chemical class, while hydroxyzine belongs to another and brompheniramine, to still another. Recently some newer antihistamines (containing terfenadine or astemizole) have been introduced that are much less sedating than some of the older ones, and there are still more such nonsedating antihistamines on the horizon.

Decongestants While antihistamines reduce the itching, sneezing and running noses for children with allergic rhinitis, they do not help a child's nasal congestion. For this, physicians suggest decongestants, which are available both over-the-counter and by prescription. These reduce a child's congestion by constricting the many tiny blood vessels in the mucous membranes lining the nose. Decongestants, however, have no effect on the basic allergic reaction involving IgE antibodies and mast cells.

Children often take decongestants by mouth; among the most common oral decongestants are ephedrine, pseudoephedrine, phenylephrine and phenylpropanolamine. "Parents should be aware that decongestants are stimulants," says Dr. Pawlowski. "Within a half-hour, your child may become more active, and this may continue for four to six hours. If it's too much, then don't use these drugs." Other possible side effects include insomnia, high blood pressure and, in some susceptible children, an increased heart rate. "Otherwise, these drugs are generally really rather safe. They are good drugs." Physicians often suggest that children take combined antihistamine-decongestant preparations.

Decongestants are also available in the form of nasal sprays; some of the common ones include phenylephrine, oxymetazoline and xylometazoline. However, as we discussed in the chapter on allergic rhinitis (see page 77), children—or adults—should not use these decongestant sprays for any longer than three to five days, because they can cause a "rebound effect," which actually makes the nose become *more* congested.

Cromolyn   Cromolyn is one of the newer anti-allergy and anti-asthma drugs; it has been in use only since the late 1960s.

In contrast to the antihistamines and decongestants, cromolyn works only as a preventative. Its action is anti-inflammatory: it stabilizes mast cells and prevents them from releasing histamine and the other biochemical substances, the mediators, that produce allergic symptoms. Cromolyn is not effective for allergies and asthma when taken by mouth:

it works only topically, that is, applied directly to the part of the body where its action is desired.

Children who have allergic rhinitis spray cromolyn into their noses to prevent symptoms. Cromolyn also comes in an ophthalmic version that physicians sometimes prescribe for allergic reactions of the eyes. Children who have asthma either spray cromolyn into their mouths from a metered-dose inhaler, with or without the help of a spacer, and then inhale it into their lungs or else they inhale the drug from a nebulizer. (See Chapter 7, pages 112–13, for descriptions of these devices, which assist people in taking anti-asthma medications.) Some children who have exercise-induced asthma regularly inhale cromolyn just before they participate in gym class or other sports to prevent acute attacks.

Cromolyn does not work quickly enough to help an acute asthma attack that is already in progress. "A common thing is that parents don't realize how cromolyn works," says Dr. Pawlowski. "It takes being on it for weeks before a child gets the maximum effect. And then it also takes weeks for the effect to disappear after a child stops using it."

Cromolyn is virtually devoid of any side effects, says the Heart, Lung Institute's 1991 Expert Panel Report on asthma. The only ones are, sometimes, some local irritation, stinging or burning or, sometimes, it can set off sneezing. "Cromolyn is one of the most benign medications that there is," says Dr. Pawlowski. "It's probably one of the safest drugs ever, of any class of drugs. And because of that, no one should really hesitate using it."

Theophylline   Theophylline has also been used for half a century, and today it is still a medication that children commonly take to combat asthma. Theophylline is a relative of caffeine in its chemical structure, and it is a bronchodilator: its effect on the lungs is to open up the bronchial airways. It accomplishes this by directly relaxing the bronchial muscles, and also, it is believed, by inhibiting the release of biochemical substances, the mediators, from mast cells.

Physicians sometimes inject theophylline intravenously in the emergency room, when a child is suffering an acute asthma attack, but more frequently children take theophylline, by mouth, regularly, day in and day out, to keep their airways open and reduce the likelihood of acute attacks. "Theophylline is a drug to be used for a maintenance regimen," says Dr. Pawlowski.

Theophylline comes in a wide variety of preparations: capsules, tablets, liquids, as well as fine, beadlike sprinkles, which children take mixed with food. Some theophylline preparations are relatively fast-acting in that the medication is released promptly into the bloodstream; other preparations release the theophylline more slowly and thus allow the child to take the medication less frequently during the day.

The main side effect of theophylline is that it acts like a cup of coffee. "When a child begins therapeutic doses of theophylline," explains Dr. Pawlowski, "it is like taking three to five cups of coffee a day, and children normally don't drink that much caffeine. And when a child goes from nothing to that, he is bound to have some stimulation." According to the Heart, Lung Institute's 1991 Expert Panel Report on asthma, "because theophylline causes central nervous stimulation, it may produce behavioral disturbances in children." Some children may be hyperactive or nervous or irritable. Some may have headaches or insomnia, nausea or diarrhea or may have to urinate more often. Physicians therefore usually start children on lower doses of theophylline than they will ultimately need and then increase the doses gradually. "It is a matter of developing tolerance," says Dr. Pawlowski. "We edge up slowly, adding one cup, so to speak, to the regimen every two or three days or more."

Recently some studies have suggested that theophylline may affect school performance in some children. However, these studies have been done only in relatively small numbers of children, and the Food and Drug Administration in a 1988 review of the reports concluded that they did not support the hypothesis of an adverse effect of theophylline on school performance.

"Theophylline has gotten bad press lately," notes Dr. Pawlowski. "People worry that it affects intellectual skills. The final word isn't in until researchers look at very, very long-term use of the drug, but in my view, I don't think there is a problem with using theophylline. Some children may be a little bit more exquisitely sensitive to it, but it's been a rare case when I've started someone on theophylline and edged up the dose slowly that a child hasn't tolerated it."

Physicians and patients do, however, have to be more careful with theophylline than with many medications, because there is a narrow range between effective and potentially toxic doses. "You need blood levels of probably at least 10 micrograms per milliliter to get reasonable effects," explains Dr. Pawlowski, "but the toxic effects start at 20 micrograms." Children taking theophylline therefore must see their physicians regularly, at least once every six months, to have the levels in their blood measured. Monitoring theophylline serum concentrations, emphasizes the 1991 Expert Panel Report on asthma, is an important part of the care of people with asthma.

"However, it is really not a major problem maintaining a child within that range," continues Dr. Pawlowski. "You calculate a child's dose on the basis of his or her weight, and then there are some known things, such as viruses or antibiotics or other drugs, that can change the drug's metabolism. Most of the time it is not difficult to adjust a child's dose within the safe range.

"Most children who have toxicity problems with theophylline are children who failed to take the drug and then when they became acutely ill, took double doses—and then were too embarrassed to tell anyone. They may get extra theophylline in the emergency room, and then when the other doses that they took get absorbed, they become toxic." Or a child on a regular visit to his physician may have a low theophylline level on his blood test, yet not admit that he failed to take the drug—and the doctor may increase his dose. "Sometimes we find children on twice the normal dose of theophylline. This is a signal that there has been a miscommunication about whether or not the child took the medication." Dr. Pawlowski emphasizes, "Parents should definitely tell the doctor if a child has missed doses of theophylline."

Adrenaline-Like Drugs The so-called beta-adrenergic drugs include epinephrine (adrenaline) and a variety of related, synthetic, adrenaline-like medications. Epinephrine is one of the natural hormones secreted by the adrenal glands that help our bodies gear up to deal with the stress of emergency situations. Epinephrine produces a broad range of effects in the body. It excites the central nervous system and stimulates the heart, causing it to pump faster and more powerfully. It increases blood pressure and pours glucose into the blood. And it also dilates the bronchial airways in the lungs.

The hormone is thus very useful in many acute allergic emergency situations. Physicians give children shots of epinephrine (or one of its relatives) to counteract life-threatening anaphylactic reactions to foods, insect venoms and drugs. And when children who have asthma have acute attacks, emergency room physicians often inject them with epinephrine.

Physicians advise that parents of children prone to severe allergic reactions to foods or insect venoms should carry a kit containing an easy-to-use, prefilled syringe of epinephrine. After Stephanie had a life-threatening reaction to walnuts in a birthday cake at her nursery school, her mother began carrying an epinephrine kit and also has given one to the school. And Marjorie, whose hand swelled up from a yellow-jacket sting, has an epinephrine kit in her kitchen and carries another whenever she thinks she might encounter a stinging insect.

Many children who have asthma also take synthetic, adrenaline-like drugs regularly, every day, to keep their bronchial airways open and to prevent episodes of acute attacks. These beta-adrenergic drugs dilate bronchial airways via biochemical pathways different from those of theophylline, and physicians often prescribe maintenance regimens that include both categories of drugs.

Some children take beta-adrenergics by mouth, either as tablets, capsules or liquids; among the oral beta-adrenergics are metaproterenol, terbutaline and albuterol. Other children take them in aerosol form, from a nebulizer or a metered-dose inhaler, with or without a spacer (see Chapter 7, pages 112–13 for a description of these devices); among the beta-adrenergics available as aerosols are the three mentioned above and also isoproterenol and isoetharine. Children who have exercise-induced asthma often take puffs from an albuterol inhaler five to ten minutes before they exercise.

And in emergency rooms and many pediatricians' offices, treatments with beta-adrenergic aerosols are replacing shots of epinephrine for children who are suffering acute attacks of asthma. Inhaled beta-adrenergics, says the 1991 Expert Panel Report on asthma, are the medications of choice for treatment of acute asthma attacks.

Common side effects of these adrenaline-like medications include muscle tremors and palpitations of the heart, and like theophylline, the drugs are stimulants. "So if a child is taking both theophylline and oral beta-adrenergics," says Dr. Pawlowski, "he or she might have more difficulty with hyperactivity." In recent years, researchers have devised a new generation of these adrenaline-like drugs that have less of a stimulating effect on the heart and more of a dilating effect on the bronchial airways. Among these newer beta-adrenergics are terbutaline and albuterol.

The adrenaline-like medications produce far fewer side effects, emphasizes Dr. Pawlowski, when a child takes them as aerosols rather than by mouth. "The inhaled route is the best. Children can still have some side effects that way, but if your child needs beta-adrenergics frequently, even the new generation, you should try to have him or her learn—at the youngest possible age—to take them by the inhaled route, to minimize the side effects."

Corticosteroids Steroids are a large family of natural body substances, with similar chemical structures, that includes cholesterol and both the female sex hormones (estrogen and progesterone) and the male sex hormone (testosterone). The infamous—and dangerous—steroids that some athletes and body-builders illegally misuse are anabolic steroids, which are relatives of testosterone; these, however, are quite different from the steroids that physicians sometimes prescribe for allergies and asthma.

The steroids that children take for allergies and asthma are *corticosteroids.* Like epinephrine (adrenaline), corticosteroids are hormones secreted by our adrenal glands to help our bodies cope with stress. Corticosteroids have wide-ranging effects on many body systems. One of their key functions is helping our body regulate glucose metabolism. As anti-allergy and anti-asthma drugs, among the many important actions of corticosteroids is their ability both to prevent and reduce tissue inflammation. They also reduce the symptoms of the IgE allergic reaction itself. Corticosteroids have been used for asthma since the 1950s and are the most powerful of the drugs available to treat allergies and asthma.

Physicians may prescribe short courses of corticosteroids (usually prednisone or methylprednisolone) by mouth for children who suffer severe acute allergic reactions to foods, stinging-insect venoms, poison ivy or drugs. When a child has a severe asthma attack, corticosteroids are among the drugs that physicians may give intravenously.

Children who have severe asthma symptoms also sometimes need to take short courses of oral corticosteroids, from time to time, for a few days or weeks, to prevent or reduce the severity of acute attacks. For children who wheeze every time they get a cold, "we may give parents five to seven days' worth of oral steroids to use at home," says Dr. Pawlowski, "and tell them to give the steroids to the child early on if their usual asthma medications are not working. That can often help abort an asthma attack or diminish its severity enough that the child doesn't have to go to the emergency room or into the hospital."

During the past decade, there has been less fear of using short courses of oral corticosteroids to treat severe, acute exacerbations of asthma, says the Expert Panel Report on asthma. "It is clear that the duration and severity of an acute [attack] can be substantially reduced by therapy with corticosteroids," says the report. Early treatment with oral corticosteroids "prevents progression of the [attack], decreases the need for emergency department visits or hospitalizations, and reduces the morbidity of the illness."

Some children with very severe asthma (as we mentioned in Chapter 7, pages 114–15) sometimes become steroid-dependent; that is, they must take oral corticosteroids more or less continuously to keep their asthma under control and to prevent acute attacks. "This is rare," says Dr. Pawlowski. "Probably less than 5 percent of children with asthma really need steroids for long periods of time."

The side effects of corticosteroids taken by mouth can be significant. "However, you really have to separate short-term use from long-term use," Dr. Pawlowski emphasizes. When an asthmatic child takes steroids for a few days when he has a cold, "for that short period of time, the side effects are really nominal." He may gain some weight due to fluid retention, show fluctuations in blood pressure or, sometimes, experience depression or euphoria. "It can elevate mood a little bit. You feel a bit better. And you might, after a couple of days, get the munchies. Your appetite is slightly stimulated. The major thing is that corticosteroids temporarily suppress the normal functioning of the adrenal gland. If the child suffers trauma or needs surgery, parents should tell the physicians the child is taking steroids so that he or she can get extra adrenal hormones."

With the less common, long-term use of oral corticosteroids, however, there can be additional, serious side effects "that have to be taken into consideration," says Dr. Pawlowski. Steroids can interfere with a child's growth. The weight gain can cause children to look puffy. "They get chubby cheeks, and the distribution of fat on their bodies is altered." They may also excrete sugar in their urine, develop ulcers, muscle weakness or osteoporosis. "Steroids sometimes stimulate acne or cause scars—stretch marks—on the skin that can be troublesome. And we have to be vigilant about cataracts; if children are on steroids for long periods, they need regular ophthalmologic exams. Some of these side effects are more reversible than others. The muscle weakness, acne, weight gain and chubby cheeks all reverse when the child stops taking the steroids. But if growth is slowed, that may not be reversible, and the stretch scars on the skin may remain for a long time."

Prolonged daily use of oral corticosteroids, says the Expert Panel Report, is reserved for people who have severe asthma. And "it is preferable," says allergist Lillian P. Kravis, M.D., of The Children's Hospital of Philadelphia, "for children to take oral corticosteroids on an alternate-day regimen."

"However," Dr. Pawlowski continues, "in the rare instances when a child is facing life-threatening asthma, or a severe impairment of his activities, so that the asthma is really diminishing his quality of life to a significant degree, there is no alternative therapy. Then you really have to balance the possible risk of these side effects against the drug's benefits in overcoming the life-diminishing aspects of the disease.

"People tend to equate the use of steroids for any length of time with all the severe side effects of this long-term use, and we spend a lot of time trying to allay parents' fears about this. Many parents are still very reluctant to give their children steroids for even short periods of time, and they probably are paying for it in terms of the severity of the child's asthma and the amount of time he or she spends in the hospital."

The corticosteroid preparations that children with asthma spray into their mouths and then inhale into their lungs are much less likely to produce any significant side effects. "Most of the possible side effects can be largely avoided by using these inhaled steroids," Dr. Pawlowski says. "Inhaled steroids can make a big difference, because much less steroid actually gets absorbed into the body. In the recommended dose, there are minimal to no side effects. And even these can be minimized if the child washes out his mouth afterward so that he doesn't swallow any of the medication." The corticosteroids that can be inhaled into the lungs for asthma include beclomethasone, triamcinolone and flunisolide, and children take them from metered-dose inhalers, with or without spacers. (See Chapter 7, pages 112–13.) Adds Dr. Kravis, "We are using steroids more and more in the inhaled form."

The corticosteroids that children with allergic rhinitis spray into their noses are even less likely to produce serious side effects. "These nasal steroids get absorbed very little," says Dr. Pawlowski, "even less than from the lungs, and the doses are a lot smaller. So from nasal steroids, once again, when they are used as they are prescribed, there's virtually no adrenal suppression, and side effects should not be a problem. They should be very, very safe." The most common side effects are sneezing or local irritation or stinging in the nose. The corticosteroids available as nasal sprays are the same three that are used in asthma inhalers: beclomethasone, triamcinolone and flunisolide. Like cromolyn, steroid nasal sprays "need a week or two before they get to maximum effectiveness. And your child should not be constantly using these nasal steroids either. He should be cycling off them periodically to assess whether or not he still really needs them."

The corticosteroids that are used directly on children's skin for eczema and poison ivy and other forms of contact dermatitis include hydrocortisone, methylprednisolone, dexamethasone and betamethasone. These come as aerosols, creams, lotions and ointments of varying strengths, some over-the-counter, some by prescription. The risk of side effects from these is very small; the most common are local itching or irritation. However, these can, in high dosages, damage the skin. If a child has "lots of very raw, inflamed skin, and uses lots of high-potency steroids for a long period of time, over a week," says Dr. Pawlowski, "and particularly if it is covered with a dressing, a significant amount of steroid may be absorbed and may cause side effects." For eczema, steroids should be used only on the lesions themselves and then just until the lesions clear up.

"One problem is that parents sometimes feel finicky about using these topical steroids and apply them erratically," continues Dr. Pawlowski. "This puts the damper on the eczema but does not totally clear it up. The objective is to totally eliminate the lesions. Often, if we apply the topical steroid three times a day, in three or four days to a week, the lesions can be healed and the child can be taken off the medication. Whereas if you piddle around with the topical steroid, you can be using it for a month and end up using much greater amounts, and the lesions may still not be resolved."

Immunotherapy (Allergy Shots)

For some types of allergies, if medications do not overcome your child's symptoms well enough, or if they cause troubling side effects, allergists can offer immunotherapy—allergy shots.

Allergy shots are available for many of the inhaled allergens that cause allergic rhinitis and trigger some children's asthma. Shots are also available for the same six stinging insects for which allergists can skin test: honeybee, yellow jacket, yellow hornet, white-faced hornet, *Polistes* paper wasp and imported fire ant.

Immunotherapy is *not* effective, however, for allergies to foods, for most forms of eczema or for asthma triggered by nonallergic mechanisms such as infections or exercise.

Allergists these days give allergy shots much less frequently than they formerly did. "The indications for the use of shots have lessened," explains Dr. Kravis, "because there are now so many more drugs to choose from. At one time allergists leaned a lot more heavily on the shots, because that was about the only treatment available." And the shots themselves have also improved. "Over the last five years, there has been a lot of progress in identifying specific allergens and purifying the extracts. The shots are more precise and work better."

Immunotherapy involves a substantial amount of time. "Some people think that as soon as a child receives one shot, he or she is going to do better," says Dr. Sweinberg. "That's not the case. Allergy shots require a big commitment." First, the allergists must establish with skin tests precisely which allergens your child is sensitive to. Then the physicians make up a mixture, specifically for your child, which contains dilute extracts of each of these allergens.

Among the inhaled allergens, shots are most effective for allergies to pollens—of the grasses, trees and weeds—and also house-dust mites. Since allergists discovered, in the 1960s, that dust mites are the major allergenic component of house dust, they less often give shots for house dust itself, which they now realize is a complex mixture of many different allergens.

Shots are generally less effective for allergies to molds. "We don't like to put the molds in serum because of questionable efficacy and because they can cause local reactions," explains Dr. Sweinberg, "but I will on occasion put them in. We take care of a lot of children who live down at the shore, and because of the dampness, mold can be their major problem."

Nor do the allergists at The Children's Hospital of Philadelphia often give shots for allergies to animals, because it is simpler and more effective for a child to avoid them. "While it is possible to desensitize to animal dander," explains Dr. Kravis, "it would not be effective if the child has continuous contact with the animal." Occasionally the allergists do include animal danders in a serum for a child who has only intermittent exposure. "Some children, usually older children, complain that they can't sleep over at their friends' homes because there are cats in the houses. They would like to have a little bit more freedom in social interaction. We hesitate to use immunotherapy in these situations, because we can't guarantee that it will offer adequate protection."

Allergists start a child's immunotherapy by injecting him or her—usually in the upper arm—with a shot of a very dilute solution of his or her treatment extract. Then the child must come back, usually at weekly intervals, for additional shots, as the allergists gradually increase the concentration of extracts in each shot, until they build up to a maintenance dose. "You are building up to the top dose for much of the first six months," emphasizes Dr. Kravis. Once the maintenance dose is reached, and if the child's symptoms abate, the allergists may lengthen the intervals between the shots.

Immunotherapy works by "building up blocking antibodies that are different from the IgE antibodies the patient has by nature that make him or her overreactive," explains Dr. Kravis. "The IgE antibodies are responsible for the allergic symptoms." The series of allergen injections gradually gives rise to antibodies of the immunoglobulin G class (IgG antibodies; see Chapter 1, page 11). Like IgE antibodies, IgG antibodies are also specific: if a child is getting shots for ragweed, he or she develops anti-ragweed IgG antibodies. These IgG antibodies are "good" antibodies, because they block the "bad" IgE antibodies and so lessen the allergic symptoms. As a child continues to get shots, the level of IgE antibodies in his body gradually declines. Immunotherapy also produces a wide variety of other changes—which are not fully understood—in the body's immune system.

A child's progress with shots can be slowed if he or she experiences any significant side effects. As with skin tests, the shots expose a child to substances to which he is sensitive and he can have an allergic reaction to the shots themselves. Again, there is a remote possibility of a life-threatening ana-phylactic reaction (see Chapter 2, pages 16–17). The same survey of allergists mentioned in the section on skin testing (see page 128) found eighteen deaths from allergy shots over a ten-year period; again, this number is probably an un-dercount, but death is very rare considering the large number of shots that allergists give every year. "The most common reactions are local ones," says Dr. Sweinberg, "and I would say they occur in certainly less than 5 percent of the children. Some children get a large hive that can encompass the arm. I've seen generalized, all-over itching. And some children de-velop respiratory reactions, wheezing or coughing. However, these are very rare events."

Because of the possibility of side effects, however, "We have the children sit in the office," says Dr. Sweinberg, "for at least twenty minutes after their shots to make sure that they are not going to have an adverse reaction."

If a child does have a side effect from a shot, the allergists then do not increase the concentration of serum for the next shot. "If we are having problems with a local reaction," says Dr. Sweinberg, "we have to repeat the dose, and it then takes longer to build up to the maintenance dose."

It takes between six months and a year to see a response to immunotherapy, and the allergists count on at least three years for a series of shots. There is no fixed program because it all depends on the child's response to the shots. "Up to 80 percent of the children," says Dr. Sweinberg, "I would say, do respond to the shots."

Janice, who has "very, very intense" allergic rhinitis from ragweed and other fall-pollinating weeds, has been contentedly taking allergy shots for about ten years now. She has no significant side effects, and she no longer needs to take any antihistamines. Her only anti-allergy medication is a nasal corticosteroid, two puffs in each nostril morning and evening. "Fall is such a beautiful season of the year, when the leaves turn," Janice says, "but I used to hate it, because I felt so dreadful." Now when fall comes, she is delighted. "I can breathe through my nose!"

CONTROVERSIAL TESTS AND TREATMENTS

Parents may sometimes come across some other, unorthodox diagnostic techniques and treatment methods that the American Academy of Allergy and Immunology says—in formal Position Statements published in *The Journal of Allergy and Clinical Immunology* (May 1981)—are of unproven value.

Cytotoxicity Testing To test whether a person is allergic to specific food and inhaled allergens, the suspect substances are each mixed with a sample of the person's whole blood or white blood cells. If the person is allergic to a particular substance, supposedly this procedure will cause the destruction of white cells. (The word "cytotoxicity" means the ability to poison cells.)

This procedure, says the academy, is "time-consuming" and "has never been proved effective . . . nor has a scientific basis for its use been demonstrated." There is no difference between the reactions in allergic and nonallergic patients.

And a Review and Position Paper from the American College of Physicians, published in the *Annals of Internal*

Medicine (February 15, 1989), agrees, stating that cytotoxicity testing "has no rational scientific basis" and "is not reliable."

Skin Titration (Rinkel Method)   In this method, doctors perform skin tests on a person using up to nine different dilutions of each allergen extract being tested.

This is a practice, says the American College of Physicians in its 1989 Review and Position Paper, "that overuses skin testing and is likely to produce nonspecific or irrelevant reactions at highest concentrations" and could "erroneously justify the use of immunotherapy . . . for patients who may not be allergic at all."

In determining the starting dose for immunotherapy, says the American Academy of Allergy and Immunology in its 1981 Position Statements, "The Rinkel method would have predicted a starting dose too low for 45 of 52 patients in one study and would have resulted in waste of time."

Sublingual Testing and Treatment   To test for allergies, a few drops of a dilute solution of each allergen, in turn, are placed under a person's tongue. (The adjective "sublingual" comes from the Latin for under the tongue.) Supposedly, if a person is allergic to a given substance, this procedure will provoke the appearance of the person's typical symptoms, usually within ten minutes.

The American College of Allergy and Immunology has evaluated sublingual provocative testing in multicenter, double-blind, controlled investigations and concluded that it does not discriminate between placebo controls and food extracts. The American College of Physicians also says in its 1989 Position Paper, "The claims that . . . sublingual provocation can identify specific allergens . . . have no scientific foundation."

Proponents of this procedure further claim that they can cause a person's allergic symptoms to disappear by administering a "neutralizing dose" of the extract that is supposedly causing them. Again, says the American Academy of Allergy and Immunology in its 1981 Position Statements, "no controlled clinical studies indicating a . . . therapeutic effect of sublingual antigen administration . . . are known to the [academy's Executive] Committee."

Subcutaneous Provocation Testing and Neutralization Treatment As with sublingual testing and treatment, proponents of this method claim that they can test a person for allergies by injecting allergen extracts under the skin to provoke the person's typical symptoms and then immediately treat the person by injecting a "neutralizing dose."

Again, the American Academy of Allergy and Immunology says, "There are no known immunologic mechanisms that can account for the 'neutralizing effects' of dilute solutions of allergenic extracts. . . . The suggestion that neutralization therapy can provide rapid relief within minutes or hours cannot be supported by controlled clinical studies or immunologic data."

Urine Immunization In this procedure, a fresh, sterilized sample of a person's own urine is injected into a muscle.

Not only does this treatment have "no rationale or immunologic basis," says the American Academy of Allergy and Immunology, but it is also "potentially dangerous" since such injections of urine could produce serious kidney disease.

CLINICAL ECOLOGY

Many of these controversial tests and treatments are employed by physicians who call themselves clinical ecologists.

Clinical ecology is an approach, says the American Academy of Allergy and Immunology in another Position Statement (published in *The Journal of Allergy and Clinical Immunology* in August 1986), that ascribes a wide range of symptoms—including behavior disorders, depression, chronic fatigue, arthritis, hypertension, learning disabilities, schizophrenia, gastrointestinal symptoms, respiratory problems and urinary complaints—to exposure to numerous common substances in the environment.

"There is no clear evidence," the academy concludes, "that many of the symptoms noted above are related to allergy, sensitivity, toxicity, or any other type of reaction from foods, water, chemicals, pollutants, viruses, and bacteria in the context presented." The concept of clinical ecology "is an unproven and experimental methodology."

CHAPTER 9

What Parents Can Do to Help

Many of the most effective measures for helping children with allergies and asthma are those that parents can—indeed, must—do themselves at home.

For one thing, you can help your children avoid the substances that cause their allergies. Avoiding whatever allergens a child is allergic to—as we have said repeatedly throughout this book—is the best treatment for any type of allergy.

Suggestions on how parents can help their children avoid allergenic foods, allergenic substances that a child might touch and allergenic venoms of stinging insects, we have discussed in the chapters about these allergies.

Here in this chapter, we offer practical tips on how you can help your children avoid the allergenic substances in the air that can cause allergic rhinitis, exacerbate eczema and trigger acute attacks of asthma in susceptible children.

At the end of this chapter, we include a listing of health organizations specializing in allergies and asthma, which parents can contact for additional information and other services.

Particularly with asthma, as we discussed in Chapter 7,

page 111, it is important to try to prevent acute attacks of the disease, stresses the 1991 Expert Panel Report on asthma from the National Heart, Lung and Blood Institute, because inflammation and swelling in the lungs can persist for weeks after an episode.

After an acute attack of asthma, explains Dr. Nicholas A. Pawlowski, Director of the Allergy Section at The Children's Hospital of Philadelphia, "a child's airways often remain more sensitive and hyperreactive—that is, extra twitchy—for a long time afterward, so that a trigger your child normally can tolerate may well bring on more spasms of the bronchial muscles and more wheezing."

The mother of seven-year-old Patrick, who has severe asthma, has noticed this phenomenon for herself. "Once Patrick's asthma is set off, it keeps on going," she says, "and it usually takes him about a week to ten days to get over it. Then the next time, it sometimes doesn't take as much to stir up his asthma again."

Each person with asthma, as we emphasized in Chapter 7, page 111, "must learn to understand his or her own set of triggers, so that he or she can learn how to avoid them when possible, or at least anticipate their consequences," says Dr. Pawlowski. "It is essential that both the parents and the child develop an understanding about how the child's triggers drive his or her asthmatic condition."

Therefore, for the majority of asthmatic children whose attacks are triggered by allergies, "environmental control to reduce exposure to indoor and outdoor [inhaled] allergens," emphasizes the Heart, Lung Institute's Expert Panel Report, "is a critical component of asthma management." Treatment for asthma is less effective, or often ineffective, the report stresses, if the asthmatic person continues to be exposed to the substances that trigger his or her attacks.

Patrick's mother says, "You just have to keep them from being near things that are going to set them off. I totally watch Patrick's environment."

Avoiding House Dust and House-Dust Mites

If your child has allergic rhinitis, eczema or asthma due to an allergy to house-dust mites, or to any of the many other allergens that can occur in house dust (cockroaches, feathers, kapok, pollens, molds and dander from cats, dogs and other pets), allergists recommend that you try aggressively to reduce the amount of dust in the house, concentrating on your child's bedroom. Dust mites tend to proliferate the most profusely in bedrooms, and it is also the room in which a child spends the most time, one third to one half of his or her life.

The greatest source of dust-mite exposure in a house is a child's bedding, which provides mites with ideal conditions of warmth, humidity and food. They feed, you recall, on human dander. Allergists suggest encasing both the mattress and the box spring in airtight, mite-proof coverings. Whether or not your child is actually allergic to feathers themselves, feathers are a favorite abode of mites. One of the common dust-mite species is called *Dermatophagoides pteronyssinus,* and *"pteronyssinus"* means "feather-loving." Allergists thus recommend replacing any feather pillows or comforters filled with down.

Carpets can also harbor dust mites, and vacuum cleaning is not sufficient to get rid of them. Allergists therefore may recommend removing any wall-to-wall carpeting from the bedroom and either leaving the floor bare or using only small, washable scatter rugs. They also suggest removing any upholstered furniture and other dust collectors—heavy curtains, wall hangings, books, knickknacks, stuffed animals and other toys—and replacing venetian blinds with window shades.

Says dust-mite expert Thomas A. E. Platts-Mills, M.D., of the University of Virginia, "Making a bedroom as easy to clean as a hospital room is both practical and highly appropriate for any mite-sensitive patient."

When Patrick was first diagnosed as having asthma, his mother knew exactly what to do because she had had asthma herself as a child. "I had a stripped-down room when I was a child. So I went ahead and took out the books and posters and banners." Mary Ann, when she was nine, found it "a good excuse to get rid of my huge heap of leftover stuffed animals." And ten-year-old Priscilla reports, "I got rid of my wool sheepskin rug. And I packed up all my little trinkets on my dresser, in ten boxes. And now my mom is looking for a glass-covered bookcase for me."

Allergists suggest washing the child's bedding, curtains and rugs frequently and also dusting the bedroom with a damp cloth and cleaning the floors with a damp mop. How often, of course, depends on how severe a child's allergies are; some families find they must do it every day. "Two years ago, when my son's asthma was so bad," says one mother, "I would spend two hours a day cleaning his room. I wiped everything down, his floor, his toys, everything in his room. That was tough, but it was worth it because I've seen such an improvement in him."

"I dust and vacuum every other day," says Judy's mother, "straight through the house. I don't move all the furniture, but I do a good job. I dust off tops of pictures. I open the windows when I clean. I try to keep dust down."

If the house has a forced hot-air heating system, which can spread mites all over a house, allergists suggest taping dust filters over the registers. And since high humidity encourages dust-mite growth, "their numbers can increase," warns allergist Sharon K. Sweinberg, M.D. of The Children's Hospital of Philadelphia, "if a vaporizer or humidifier is used during the winter."

Allergists suggest that parents try these rigorous dust-reducing strategies for at least several months. Some parents find that these methods do not help their child's allergies enough to be worth the considerable trouble. One mother found that her daughter felt so uncomfortable in her stripped-down room that she would not stay in it at night. "She would drag her sleeping bag into her brother's room. And at this point, I was trying to reason with a seven-year-old!" And some families discover that less herculean measures suffice. One man found that simply encasing the mattress and box spring in heavy, rubberized covers kept the house-dust mites under enough control for him.

AVOIDING ANIMAL DANDERS

If your child is allergic to your family cat, dog, bird or other animal, allergists flatly advise: get rid of the animal. "If it is a pet," says allergist Lillian P. Kravis, M.D., of The Children's Hospital of Philadelphia, "then it's pretty obvious what parents should do. It would be best, of course, to remove the animal completely.

"However, sometimes we have to compromise," Dr. Kravis continues, "because the parents and child are absolutely devastated by that suggestion. That's a touchy problem."

"When Judy developed asthma, we did have a dog," says her mother. Judy had a positive skin test to dogs, and the family decided to remove the dog from the house. "It was really heart-breaking. I had raised the dog from a puppy. It's like giving away one of your kids. But my brother-in-law took the dog, so we do get reports on how he is doing."

One obvious strategy is to substitute another kind of animal. When one family realized that their daughter was allergic to cats, they got a golden retriever instead. However, warns Dr. Sweinberg, "This may not be the best solution. A child allergic to one furry or feathered animal may often develop allergies to others." The 1991 Expert Panel Report on asthma points out that all warm-blooded animals, including birds, can cause allergic reactions, and that "there is no non-allergenic dog; short-haired dogs are just as allergenic as those with longer hair." Patrick, whose asthma is triggered by allergies to cats *and* dogs, among other things, has decided, his mother reports, "that maybe he should have some gold-fish."

Another possibility is to separate your child from the pet for a trial period of time to find out whether or not your child's allergic symptoms improve. "If your child's condition repeatedly improves whenever he is away from home for several days," notes Dr. Pawlowski, "this certainly demonstrates the pet's role in triggering his symptoms. With a child who has asthma, parents can monitor whether or not the child improves through the daily use of a peak-flow meter (see Chapter 7, pages 116–17; and also page 164).

In a recent study at Johns Hopkins University, however, physicians discovered that when a cat is removed from a house, its allergenic dander can persist in the house for a surprisingly prolonged period of time. The Johns Hopkins researchers concluded in their article in *The Journal of Allergy and Clinical Immunology* (April 1989), that "any trial of less than four to six months may be inadequate and, in some instances, even that may not be long enough." Removing carpets, the researchers found, could hasten the disappearance of the offending cat allergens.

Some people find that they can make do by banishing a pet outdoors or otherwise minimizing their exposure to the animal. Barbara, who is allergic, she says, to "everything except goats," nevertheless insists on having dogs. She currently has two: a border collie and a Norwegian elkhound. "The issue is how can you live with two dogs so that it minimizes the allergies. I just have to minimize contact with them physically. I have to be real careful, when I touch them, not to touch my eyes. And the bedroom is off base for dogs. They are not in the bedroom. They are not in my bed."

Individual cats and dogs do vary in their ability to cause allergic reactions, as mentioned earlier in Chapter 4, page 66. "I have found that I can tolerate calicoes," says one woman. "But I am very careful. I never pick up a cat. Once in a while I pick one up and put it outside, and they are always astounded. Occasionally, I do pet them, and then I always wash my hands afterward."

Since the allergenic substances produced by cats occur in their urine (as well as in their saliva and on their skin and fur), litter boxes in a home could be an important source of exposure. It is a good idea for someone other than a child or adult with a cat allergy to empty the litter box.

Allergists at Washington University in St. Louis suggest that washing the cat regularly may help. In a study of ten cats, they found that washing them for ten minutes in lukewarm water once a month "markedly reduced the production of Fel D 1, the major allergen in cats." The question is, of course, how to persuade the cat to go along with this idea. The researchers anesthetized the animals for their study, but they point out that owners of show cats wash them regularly and say that if you start when a cat is a kitten, you can train him or her to accept this regimen.

Avoiding Molds

If your child is allergic to indoor molds, which can also find their way into house dust, reducing the dust in your child's bedroom (as discussed on pages 151–53) should help. Allergists also recommend that parents scout their houses for leaks or damp areas and get them repaired. "Ordinarily it is possible to determine what the source of the mold is," notes Dr. Kravis. "There has to be dampness in a house for mold to grow. Parents will often notice that there is a leak in a closet or a room where the wallpaper is getting damp."

Parents can remove molds from the surfaces of shower stalls, bathroom tiles, plumbing fixtures, garbage cans and food storage areas by scrubbing them with a solution of laundry bleach or disinfectant. "There are a number of chemicals that destroy mold," says Dr. Kravis. "And there are also some other chemicals that can be added to paint or sprayed on furniture."

Molds can also thrive in vaporizers and humidifiers, and allergists advise that parents of children with mold allergies not use these devices in their houses. Indeed, allergists recommend using a *de*humidifier to dry out the air if there is excessive humidity in any area of the house. "Be sure to use one of adequately large capacity," adds Dr. Pawlowski. *(Consumer Reports* magazine evaluated brands of dehumidifiers in its July 1990 issue.) Improving the ventilation in a basement or other room may also help.

Molds can grow in houseplants, but, says Dr. Kravis, "Houseplants are a problem only if they are very abundant, and certainly if they are concentrated in an allergic child's bedroom. If you take care of them well and turn over and aerate the soil, that accumulation of mold is often greatly decreased."

Outdoors, molds tend to proliferate in piles of dead leaves and other decaying vegetation, and allergists suggest that parents keep their lawns mowed and grounds cleaned up and also trees and bushes trimmed away from the house to improve air circulation. Janice, who is allergic to molds, has learned to let others rake up the leaves and tidy up the yard. And Patrick's mother keeps him away from the areas in parks where leaves are piled up. "We also have to be real careful with the mulch we use around our shrubs," she adds. "We plan to use a special mulch that doesn't grow molds and won't bother Patrick, we hope."

AVOIDING POLLENS

If your child is allergic to pollens, there is nothing that you can do, of course, to eliminate them from the outdoor air, but "air conditioning the child's bedroom," Dr. Kravis points out, "and keeping the windows in the room closed reduces the child's exposure to outdoor pollens for a significant number of hours." Air conditioning also decreases a child's exposure to outdoor molds, and air conditioning in an automobile reduces exposure to both pollens and molds while a family is on the road.

"Air conditioners are one of the primary recommendations for a child who wheezes or coughs during the pollen season," adds Dr. Pawlowski. "They make a bedroom a good safe place for someone who has pollen asthma."

Allergists also advise that an allergic child stay indoors more during times when pollens are the most abundant. "Wind-borne pollens are released in greater numbers between sunrise and 9 A.M.," notes Dr. Kravis. Pollen levels also tend to be higher on windy days, and Patrick's mother makes a point of keeping him inside on those days. "I will say, Patrick, how about if we watch a video today or play a game instead of being outside."

Many allergic people also stay indoors whenever anyone in the neighborhood is mowing the lawn. "If grass is being cut in the neighborhood," says Mrs. J., "I keep Patrick in for an hour or so afterward. Or my husband will take him over to the playground to pitch ball." Mrs. J. and other mothers have campaigned to persuade schools to mow the lawns during hours when the children are not there. One high school teacher who has allergic rhinitis herself notices, "When they cut the grass during school hours, the nurse's office is full of students coming in with weeping eyes and runny noses. It's a regular little trail."

Mrs. J. has even scheduled Patrick's birthday party around the pollen season. "He loves to go to the park, and of course our county park is loaded with trees. So we had his birthday party early in the spring, before the trees came out, and everybody wore their winter coats. He won't go back to that park again until the first week in December."

Some people with significant pollen allergies take their vacations during their high allergy season, choosing a place they have discovered works for them. There is no one location, however, that is good for everyone. Some people find they have less trouble with their allergies at the seashore— but one girl suffered her first attack of asthma while visiting relatives at the New Jersey shore. Some people do well in the dry air of the American West—but Suzanne experienced her worst bout of sneezing ever while traveling high in the Colorado Rockies. "If I had been driving a car," she says, "I would have had to pull over to the side of the road."

The fact that no one place is best for everyone is one reason why allergists warn parents against moving to another part of the country just to help a child's allergies. What can happen is that even if a new place is better for a child's allergies at first, after a few years he or she may very well develop new allergies to the indigenous molds and pollens in the new environment. Americans often say their allergies are better while they are traveling in Europe—but people who live in Europe know that there are plenty of pollens and other allergenic substances floating in the air over that continent. It just takes a little time for a visitor's immune system to develop IgE antibodies against the new allergens.

THE DANGERS OF PASSIVE SMOKING

One very important thing that you can do, however, to help a child with allergies to pollens, mites and other inhaled substances is to stop smoking or at least do it outdoors or in another room. Secondhand tobacco smoke, from so-called "passive smoking," can irritate nasal membranes and lungs and aggravate allergic rhinitis and asthma in sensitive children.

Michael, who has such severe asthma, finds that when people around him smoke, "it gets me wheezing." On his job, his co-workers have designated one room as the place where other employees can smoke. "If I have to go into that one room," Michael explains, "I try not to inhale the smoke much. I just try to take short breaths until I can get out of there."

According to the 1986 Surgeon General's report *The Health Consequences of Involuntary Smoking,* it is unknown "whether exposure to environmental cigarette smoke can induce asthma in children," that is, whether a parent's smoking can actually *cause* a child to develop asthma in the first place. However, the report continues, the existing studies "suggest that maternal cigarette smoking may influence the severity of [a child's] asthma."

This Surgeon General's report also found that children of parents who smoke have more frequent respiratory infections than other children; this is particularly true for children under two years of age. Infants of smoking parents are more likely to be hospitalized for bronchitis and pneumonia during their first year of life. And children of smoking parents, the report further found, also have slightly lower scores on pulmonary-function tests (see Chapter 7, pages 109–10).

"What future respiratory burden these findings may represent for these children later in life is not known," says C. Everett Koop, M.D., former Surgeon General and Surgeon-in-Chief Emeritus at The Children's Hospital of Philadelphia, in this 1986 report. "I strongly urge parents to refrain from smoking in the presence of children as a means of protecting not only their children's current health status but also their own."

The Heart, Lung Institute's 1991 Expert Panel Report on asthma agrees: "Tobacco smoke . . . should not be in the environment of the person with asthma. An increased incidence of asthma has been reported in children who live in a home where the mother smokes. In addition, children with asthma who are exposed to maternal smoking have been shown to have . . . a higher requirement for medication . . . and more frequent emergency department visits." It is essential that people with asthma not smoke themselves, says the report, and that their exposure to passive smoking be eliminated as much as possible.

And Dr. Kravis strongly concurs, "That's one big thing we are trying to emphasize in families where there are smokers. It is a big problem."

HELPING YOUR CHILD WITH ASTHMA

Asthma, as a chronic disease like diabetes, is a disease that a child and his or her family must live with for years. "Much of the day-to-day responsibility for managing asthma," emphasizes the 1991 Expert Panel Report on asthma, "falls on the patient and the patient's family."

"Both the parents and the child," adds Dr. Pawlowski, "should make sure they thoroughly understand the disease and its treatment. This will help to diminish their fears, allow them to feel positive and comfortable about the illness and also improve their compliance with the treatment. Parents should ask questions of the child's physician and not accept treatment without adequate explanation. Yet it is still all too common for parents to have a poor understanding of their child's disease and treatment."

The Expert Panel report emphasizes that it is important for children (and adults) who have asthma "to take preventive medicine regularly and consistently." Nevertheless, says Dr. Steven M. Selbst, Director of the Emergency Department at The Children's Hospital of Philadelphia, "There are a lot of children who are supposed to be on asthma medications but who don't take them. It's a pretty common reason for them to come to the emergency room. There are some children who are in and out of here so often; they come to the emergency room a few times a month and get admitted to the hospital a few times a year. In a lot of cases, it is due to their not taking their medicine."

Also, Dr. Pawlowski continues, "There are a lot of parents who—for whatever reason—use the emergency room for primary medical care. These children tend not to do as well and make up a large portion of the patients whom we have to admit to the hospital for their asthma."

It is also important that children take their asthma medications correctly. With metered-dose inhalers, using them properly can be tricky. You should make sure that your physician checks out your child's technique. When Judy was constantly having asthma attacks, says her mother, it turned out that one factor was that she was not using the inhalers correctly. "It does take practice for a child to get it right," says Dr. Pawlowski, "so that he or she makes sure to get all the medicine into the lungs."

Communicate with Schools   Sometimes, you may find, there are problems with schools when a child needs to take asthma medications during the day. Some schools forbid children to keep their inhalers or other medications with them in their classrooms and require that the child leave the room and go to a nurse's or other office to take their medications. "But I have found that the nurse is not always there," says one mother. "She is not there more than she is there."

The American Academy of Allergy and Immunology has officially addressed this problem in a 1989 Position Statement: "For many students with asthma to function normally at school, these prescribed medications must be readily accessible. . . . School policies that require inhalers to be kept in school official's or nurse's offices result in an interference in the medical needs of the patient and may seriously delay treatment. . . . We recommend that students with asthma be permitted to have in their possession inhaled medications for the treatment and the prevention of asthma symptoms when they are prescribed by that student's physician."

"Fostering communication between the child's physician and the school," suggests Dr. Pawlowski, "is one thing that parents can do to help improve the school staff's understanding and acceptance of the child's need for treatment during the day."

"School personnel are often frightened of asthma episodes," the Expert Panel Report points out, "and are rarely well prepared to cope with them. As a result, children are sometimes barred from sports or from taking medications at school. Parents should communicate with classroom and physical education teachers, the school nurse and the principal about the child's asthma." A letter from the child's physician can be helpful. Such a letter should include, says the report, a description of your child's condition, his or her medication schedule and guidelines for responding to any symptoms.

Encourage Exercise Parents of children with asthma should also encourage them to exercise and be as active as possible. "A lot of children try to use asthma as an excuse for getting out of gym," notes Dr. Sweinberg. "I am very reluctant to write a gym excuse for a child; I am very strict about that. I will write that the child should be allowed to rest during an activity if he or she develops symptoms; that alone is often enough to take care of the asthma. I tell the children that there is some type of activity they can participate in. Swimming is one of the best; it is well tolerated by most children who have asthma.

"There is no reason why asthma should hold most children back," Dr. Sweinberg continues. "Granted, there are a handful of children who cannot participate, and sometimes children need extra medication to get them through those activities; a lot of children use their inhalers before they exercise. But it is not good to have your child sit on the sidelines when he or she can participate just as well as everybody else can."

Patrick, despite his severe asthma, nevertheless swims on a community team and enjoys downhill skiing with his family in the winter. Thirteen-year-old Mary Ann also swims competitively, and Peter, who has exercise-induced asthma, plays on three different teams, you recall: soccer, lacrosse and ice hockey. And even twenty-year-old Michael, who has such severe asthma, in between going to college and working part time, says, "I do exercises and lift weights and work out with my friends at school."

For her book *Asthma & Exercise,* Olympic-swimmer Nancy

Hogshead located athletes with asthma who had competed in the Olympics in rowing, cycling, cross-country skiing, the luge, shot put, pole vault, discus and javelin-throwing, hurdles and the fifteen-hundred-meter and one-mile races, among other sports. She also found a professional basketball player with asthma, a dancer with a professional dance company and a physician who has run both the Boston and New York marathons with his inhaler in his hand.

Recognize Early Symptoms It is important to start treating an acute attack of asthma early in its course, emphasizes the Heart, Lung Institute's Expert Panel Report on asthma, because early treatment is the most effective. "Starting (or increasing) anti-asthma medications at the first sign of [an attack] may stop an episode quickly or keep it from becoming severe. . . . It is easier and takes less medicine to stop an episode in its early phase than later." Patients should "recognize and treat even mild symptoms, because these symptoms may be early signs of a more serious episode."

To avoid delay in starting anti-asthma therapy, stresses the Expert Panel Report, the initial treatment of an asthma attack can begin at home.

It is therefore also important that parents and children, both, learn how to spot the subtle, early symptoms of an oncoming attack. "First and foremost," stresses Dr. Pawlowski, "parents should learn how to recognize an attack, what to expect and what to do about it."

From long experience, the mother of fourteen-month-old David has learned this lesson for herself. "The big thing with asthma," she explains, "is that you have to recognize the signs before it becomes an attack. That is the main thing. With David, I listen to his chest. A couple of times a day, I put my ear down to his chest and listen, and I also listen to his back. I don't make a big deal out of it, but I am in tune to how he is breathing."

Different children, however, have different early warning

symptoms. Some children cough persistently. Some become aware of a tight feeling in their chest or realize that they are short of breath. Sometimes a child's nose or chin will start to itch. "A lot of times, my children will get a light blue discoloration under their eyes," says one mother who has *two* children with asthma. "Early signs of airflow obstruction vary according to the individual," says the Expert Panel Report, "and should be identified for each patient."

Nevertheless, even adults with asthma are often unable to detect when their symptoms are getting worse. In one study, twenty-two people, aged sixteen to forty-five, who were recovering from acute attacks, believed that they were free from symptoms when, in fact, objective lung-function tests revealed that their breathing remained markedly abnormal.

"Poor perception of the severity of asthma on the part of the patient and physician," says the Expert Panel Report, "has been cited as a major factor causing delay in treatment and thus may contribute to increased severity and mortality from asthma exacerbations."

Therefore, the Expert Panel Report suggests that children with moderate or severe asthma who are five years old or more might use a *peak-flow meter* to monitor their own breathing at home. As discussed in Chapter 7, pages 116–17, some children use peak-flow meters regularly, every morning and every night, to measure their breathing, each time writing down on a chart the number of liters of air they can expel and comparing the number with what is normal for their age and size or with their own best record. This, says the report, can "help patients see patterns of triggers and symptoms as well as response to therapy." These children and their parents often have standing instructions from their physician to increase certain medications by certain amounts and also to call the physician if their peak-flow-meter reading drops below a certain level.

"Parents should be particularly alert for early signs of an acute asthma episode when children have colds or the flu," warns the Expert Panel Report. "Some children have an established pattern in which their asthma gets bad very quickly every time they get a cold. For these patients, it may be appropriate to start oral corticosteroid treatment at the earliest sign of a cold or the flu rather than waiting for acute asthma symptoms to develop. This treatment should only be started under the supervision of a physician."

The Expert Panel Report further suggests that "each patient should have available and be familiar with a written asthma plan to be followed in the event of an exacerbation of asthma." These written guidelines should include, says the report, instructions about the doses and frequencies of medications and when to change them, adverse effects to report to the physician, criteria for initiating treatment at home, steps to take in managing an acute episode and also specific criteria for seeking emergency medical care.

OTHER SOURCES OF HELP

There are a number of organizations that offer information, publications and other services to help parents of children with allergies and asthma.

American Academy of Allergy and Immunology
611 East Wells Street
Milwaukee, WI 53202
1-414-272-6071

The academy is a professional organization of allergists and clinical immunologists.

For the public, the academy publishes a quarterly newsletter, *Asthma & Allergy Advocate;* an eight-page booklet on *Adverse Reactions to Foods, A Patient's Guide to Problem Foods, Food Additives, Diagnosis, Treatment* ($0.75); a pamphlet on *Stinging Insect Allergy;* and a series of nineteen "Tips" pamphlets ($0.50 each). The pamphlet titles include *Adverse Reactions to*

Food Additives; Anaphylaxis; Atopic Dermatitis; Hives; Allergic Contact Dermatitis; Allergic Rhinitis and Nonallergic Rhinitis; Childhood Asthma; Asthma and the Schoolchild; Understanding the Pollen & Mold Season; and *Removing House Dust & Other Allergic Irritants from Your Home.*

The academy has also produced five patient-education videotapes: *The Bees Knees* (on insect allergy); *The Environment, Allergies & You; I'm Wonderful and I Have Asthma; Immunotherapy—Old Fashioned or Futuristic?;* and *A Visit to the Allergy Doctor.*

For people with food allergies, the academy has compiled a list of cookbooks and other books on the subject. Parents can obtain this list by writing the academy at the above address.

Parents can also phone 1-800-822-ASMA (2762) for more information about allergies and asthma or for a referral to an allergist in their own area.

American College of Allergy and Immunology
800 East Northwest Highway, Suite 1080
Palatine, IL 60067
1-708-359-2800

The college is another professional organization of allergists and clinical immunologists. Among their activities for physicians, the college sponsors an International Food Allergy Symposium every three years.

For the public, the college publishes *Advice from Your Allergist,* a series of one-page information sheets on single subjects. Among the topics covered recently have been food allergies, urticaria (hives), allergic rhinitis, allergy to house-dust mites, antihistamines and theophylline.

For people with asthma, the college sponsors periodic, regional Asthma Patient Conferences. These are educational workshops, conducted by allergists, to help people learn more about the disease. In 1990, for instance, the college held four of these conferences, in Washington, D.C., Dallas, Los Angeles and San Francisco.

Phone 1-800-842-7777 for copies of the information sheets and other information. Phone 1-708-359-2800 for a referral to an allergist in your area.

American Lung Association
1740 Broadway
New York, NY 10019-4374
1-212-315-8700

Founded in 1904 to help fight tuberculosis, the American Lung Association today is interested in all lung diseases, including asthma. The association's research and public-education programs are supported by the sale of Christmas Seals and other voluntary contributions. The organization has 130 affiliated, local Lung Associations in all 50 states and in Puerto Rico and the Virgin Islands. There are 19 local Lung Associations in California, for instance, 13 in Pennsylvania and 10 in New York State. The association also has a medical section, the American Thoracic Society.

Among the materials that the Lung Association offers to the public are booklets (the titles include *About Asthma; Asthma—the Facts; Controlling Asthma; The Asthma Handbook; There Are Solutions for the Student with Asthma;* and *Occupational Asthma);* a color film, *A Regular Kid;* teaching guides and posters about asthma for schools; and Superstuff, an educational kit about asthma for children from ages seven to twelve, which includes puzzles, a board game, posters, riddles, stickers and stories.

Many local Lung Associations sponsor summer camps for children with asthma and also conduct educational workshops about asthma for children and parents and for school personnel.

Look in the telephone directory for your area for the address and telephone number of your nearest local Lung Association.

Asthma and Allergy Foundation of America
1717 Massachusetts Avenue, NW, Suite 305
Washington, DC 20036
1-202-265-0265

In addition to its national headquarters in Washington, D.C., the foundation has ten chapters (in Los Angeles, St. Louis, Kansas City, Omaha, Chicago, Michigan, New England, southeastern Pennsylvania, Maryland and Florida) and dozens of local support groups and affiliates.

The $25 annual membership fee includes a membership in the nearest chapter. Members also receive a bimonthly newsletter, *Asthma and Allergy ADVANCE,* which alternates with a bimonthly bulletin called *Advance PLUS.*

Among the materials the foundation distributes are pamphlets ($0.75 each) on *Food Allergy, Adverse Reactions to Food; Skin Allergy; Hay Fever; Poison Ivy Allergy; Stinging Insect Allergy; Drug Allergy; Exercise and Asthma;* and a *Handbook for Asthmatics;* and videotapes ($20 each) on *Allergic Rhinitis; Asthma and Allergies in the School;* and *Auxiliary Inhalation Devices.*

The foundation also offers two educational programs: Asthma Care Training for Kids (ACT), for children age seven to twelve and their parents, and Childhood Asthma: Learning to Manage (CALM), for three different age groups.

Phone 1-800-7ASTHMA for more information and for referrals to physicians and to find out how to contact the foundation's nearest chapter or support group.

Mothers of Asthmatics, Inc./The National Allergy and
Asthma Network
10875 Main Street, Suite 210
Fairfax, VA 22030
1-703-385-4403

Mothers of Asthmatics was founded in 1985 by Nancy
Sander (whose own daughter Brooke has severe
asthma) to help other parents of asthmatic children.
Membership in the organization currently costs $25 a
year.

Members receive a monthly newsletter, *The MA Report,* which includes, among its articles, reviews of new
books in the field, a periodic "Ask the Doctor" column
and evaluations of allergy products such as mite-proof
covers for mattresses and special vacuum cleaners for
dust.

The organization also sells an "Asthma Organizer"
($20); *A User's Guide to Peak Flow Monitoring* ($5.00); a
twelve-page booklet, *What Everyone Needs to Know
about Theophylline* ($1.50); and for children, *I'm a
Meter Reader* ($5.00) and *So You Have Asthma Too!*
($5.00), written from the perspective of seven-year-old
Brooke Sander. This latter also comes in a video version
($12.95) for children.

National Heart, Lung and Blood Institute
9000 Rockville Pike
Bethesda, MD 20892
1-301-496-4000

One of the eleven institutes of the United States Public Health Service's National Institutes of Health, the
Heart, Lung Institute both performs and sponsors research on cardiovascular and respiratory diseases, including asthma.

For the public, the Heart, Lung Institute publishes an
eight-page brochure, *Facts About Asthma,* and an

Asthma "I.Q." quiz. To get these publications and also to get an asthma reading and resource list and other information, write the institute's National Asthma Education Program, 4733 Bethesda Avenue, Suite 530, Bethesda, MD 20814.

Copies of the National Asthma Education Program's 1991 Expert Panel Report for physicians, *Guidelines for the Diagnosis and Management of Asthma* (which we have cited so often in the asthma sections of this book), are available from this same address or phone 1-301-951-3260.

The Heart, Lung Institute also has produced four teaching manuals for running educational programs for children and their parents: *Open Airways* ($25), for inner-city children aged four to twelve; *Living with Asthma* ($40), for children eight to thirteen; *Air Power* ($10), for children nine to twelve; and *Air Wise* ($16), for individual sessions with a single child. These manuals are available from the Superintendent of Documents; United States Government Printing Office; Washington, DC 20402.

National Institute of Allergy and Infectious Diseases
9000 Rockville Pike
Bethesda, MD 20892
1-301-496-4000

The Allergy Institute is another of the eleven institutes that make up the National Institutes of Health. This institute conducts and sponsors research on infectious disease and disorders of the immune system, including asthma and the allergic diseases.

For the public, the Allergy Institute publishes a series of free booklets on allergic disorders, including *Poison Ivy Allergy; Dust Allergy; Mold Allergy; Asthma; How to Create a Dust-free Bedroom;* and *Drug Allergy.*

To obtain copies of these booklets and other information about allergies, phone the Allergy Institute's Office of Communications at 1-301-496-5717 or write the office at the above address, Building 31, Room 7A-32.

National Jewish Center for Immunology and
Respiratory Medicine
1400 Jackson Street
Denver, CO 80206
1-303-388-4461

National Jewish was founded in 1899 by Jewish philanthropists to take care of poor people with tuberculosis. Today National Jewish is a nonsectarian, medical referral center specializing in the study and treatment of chronic respiratory, immunologic and allergic diseases, including asthma, food allergies and eczema.

For the public, National Jewish publishes a series of free booklets. Among their many titles are *Eczema/ Atopic Dermatitis; Allergic and Nonallergic Rhinitis; Allergy Testing; Asthma; Your Child and Asthma; Asthma Triggers; Exercise and Asthma; Nocturnal Asthma; Healthy Breathing; Reading List—Asthma; Metered Dose Inhalers; Cleaning Nebulizers; Cromolyn; Steroids;* and *Theophylline Questions and Answers.*

Phone 1-800-222-LUNG (355-LUNG in the Denver metropolitan area) for copies of these booklets and also for other information about asthma and allergies. This LUNG LINE, as it is called, is staffed by specially trained nurses.

CHAPTER 10

Psychological Aspects of Allergies and Asthma

If your child has significant allergies or asthma, you may find that he sometimes runs into some social or psychological problems because of his disorder. This situation is not unique to children with these allergic disorders; it tends to be true of any child with any chronic disease.

Only a very, very tiny percentage of allergic and asthmatic children, however, ever have such problems significantly enough that parents need to seek professional help from a psychologist or psychiatrist.

Missing Out on Activities You may find that your child must sometimes miss out on social and other activities that other children take for granted. Five-year-old Stephanie, for example—because she has life-threatening allergies to nuts, sesame seeds, cow's milk and eggs—cannot eat the same food that the other children at her nursery school eat. She must therefore carry her own snacks to school every day. And when she goes to a birthday party, she has to be careful about what she eats. "It's hard for Stephanie," her mother notices, "to go to a party and not to be able to eat what the other children are eating."

Seven-year-old Patrick—who has serious asthma triggered by molds, animal danders and cigarette smoke—often must miss birthday parties altogether. "This weekend Patrick has been invited to a party," his mother explains, "but the little boy has a big dog, and his mother is a chain smoker. There is no way that Patrick can go to that party."

One woman recalls that when she was growing up, she was never allowed to go to the beach in August with the other children, because she always had a "summer cold." It was years later that she and her family learned that her seasonal sniffles and runny nose were not due to colds but to an allergy to ragweed pollen.

And twenty-year-old Michael—who has severe asthma triggered by allergies to many pollens—has learned that he must be careful about the timing of his outdoor excursions. Last August he and his family had to come home early from a camping trip along the Delaware River; he started wheezing, and there was no place to plug in his nebulizer. "And my little brother had a hay fever attack and took so much antihistamine he slept most of the day. My dad said, 'One's wheezing, and one's sneezing!' Next time," Michael laughs, "maybe we should go in the winter."

Impact on Self-Esteem If your child has allergic rhinitis, he may find it awkward or embarrassing to be clutching a tissue constantly and blowing his nose all the time. Children don't like to be different from other children. "You want so much to be like every other child," one grown-up recalls. "You want to be 'normal.' I grew up always feeling frustrated, because I always had a stuffy nose and couldn't breathe through my nose the way other kids did. It definitely does have an impact on your self-esteem."

Children with eczema on exposed parts of their body may understandably be self-conscious about their appearance. Dorothy, who had conspicuous eczema on her face and hands when she was in junior high school, remembers, "I used to wear my hair over my face to hide it, and high collars and long sleeves even in summer. But you can't wear high collars all the time, and it's hard to hide your hands. And you know how kids are. They'd say, 'Oooooh! What's that on your face?' I just told them that it was a rash. I wanted to brush it off; I didn't want to get into a big discussion about it.

"And some people are afraid that you are contagious; occasionally I was snubbed. In school, there were some kids who didn't want to sit next to me, or a kid would say, 'I don't want to hold your hand' or 'I don't want to be your partner.' "

Coping with Skeptics Because people with allergies and asthma look perfectly normal most of the time, your child may find that he has a credibility problem. He—and you—may run into people who do not believe in the reality of his problem. "We live in a very small town," notes Stephanie's mother, "and people here are not familiar with food allergies." Despite Stephanie's life-threatening episode in nursery school (Chapter 2, pages 33–34), "they think that I am overreacting about her allergies."

Sometimes even members of your own family may not understand. Another mother, whose son suffers from severe asthma, reports, "My mother-in-law is very much opposed to Tommy's asthma. She tells my husband that this is all a bunch of nonsense. She doesn't know of anybody else who has asthma like this, so therefore Tommy can't have it."

Your child may also have to cope with friends and relatives who tell him, "It's all in your head." Again and again, allergic people say, they are advised, "If you just ignore it, if you just don't think about it, it won't happen. You won't sneeze." Or "You won't wheeze."

One high school teacher with severe allergic rhinitis, who has been trying to persuade the maintenance people not to cut the grass during school hours, reports, "There are three of us on the faculty who have this problem and also many students. The former superintendent was very sympathetic, because he had had asthma as a child. This superintendent is not sympathetic. He has never had any kind of allergy, and he thinks this is all in our minds."

Effects on Schooling   Allergic disorders can significantly interfere with your child's education. Asthma causes children to miss more school than any other chronic disease; and allergic rhinitis and asthma, between them, are responsible for some 8 million days of school absences every year.

And even when a child does attend school, these conditions can hinder his or her ability to learn. They can cause a child to sleep poorly, because he has trouble breathing, and the fatigue can make it hard for him to concentrate on his studies. The ear infections that so commonly accompany allergic rhinitis can interfere with a child's hearing and thus potentially affect the development of his or her speech. And some asthmatic children are so distracted and anxious in school that they spend an excessive amount of time in the nurse's office and miss out on much classroom work.

CHILDREN WITH SEVERE ASTHMA HAVE THE MOST PROBLEMS

Among children with allergies and asthma, the ones who have the greatest psychological problems are, not surprisingly, the children with asthma, which is the most serious of the allergic disorders. "And those who have the most trouble, obviously, are the ones who have very severe asthma, the ones who really cannot lead a normal, unimpeded life," says Dr. Madelaine Nathanson, Ph.D., a clinical psychologist at the Philadelphia Child Guidance Clinic (affiliated with The Children's Hospital of Philadelphia) who has worked extensively with children with allergies and asthma. The children with problems serious enough to need consultations with Dr. Nathanson are, she says, "overwhelmingly asthmatic children and their families, rather than children just with allergies." Fortunately, these severe asthmatics are a very small proportion of all children with asthma.

Impact of the Initial Diagnosis When parents first learn that a child has significant asthma, this may well "throw a family into a certain degree of disarray," says Dr. Nathanson. "You must get reorganized to include the asthma." The medical regimens that some children must follow can be very complex; your child may have to take three or four different types of medications two or three times every day. "You are going to have to ferry the child to and from doctor's appointments more often, and you may have to learn how to cope with emergency situations."

You may well "feel overwhelmingly frightened and guilty," Dr. Nathanson continues. "Parents worry that they have passed this on to their children genetically, and they are troubled by that. It's very important that you be reassured that this is nothing to feel guilty about. You also need to know that there is nothing that anyone has definitively unearthed, in terms of research, that suggests there is anything in a parent's or child's character or personality that causes asthma."

Parents also "worry about their own behavior and how it affects the child. When there are clear triggers for a child's asthma attacks, such as cat dander or dust or smoking, that must be controlled, there can be large implications for a family. It can often be a conflict: your child may be really taxed by the presence of a cat in a home, and yet the family just can't give it up. It isn't lightly that people say, 'This is our family cat and that is too bad,' or 'This is all the time I can spend vacuuming.' It is with some psychological cost."

If the initial diagnosis of asthma is made when a child is an infant, "there really can be some kind of interruption of parent-infant attachment," says Dr. Nathanson. "To the extent that the diagnosis is frightening or off-putting or anxiety-provoking, that key parent-infant attachment can be disturbed in some way. If parents see the child as a source of stress, they react to him or her differently.

"Sometimes families need to reexamine their values. Ideas that they all thought they held in common may not, in fact, be so commonly held. Instead of being a track star, an asthmatic child may have to be rerouted to something else. This might very well raise issues for some families."

A diagnosis of asthma in a child "is going to affect everybody in your family," Dr. Nathanson emphasizes. "It's not something that just affects Susie. There is a certain amount of upheaval; it's not unlike any other big family event. For your family to feel that they are reeling a little bit, in the days and weeks that follow the initial diagnosis, is somewhat predictable. You should expect a period of adjustment and a certain amount of anxiety in figuring out how to proceed. That's normal.

"The overall goal is to help your child gain a sense of control over his or her symptoms and achieve the proper balance of anxiety about the illness, neither too much nor too little. If anxiety is too high, it is hypervigilance. If anxiety is too low, it leads to disregarding symptoms.

"It *will* settle down, and the way to help it settle down is just to talk about it. Keep talking with your spouse about what's going on, if one or the other of you is troubled about something. Talk with your doctor about what's worrying you. And get professional help if you need it." This could be in the form of individual, group or family counseling or therapy from either a psychologist or a psychiatrist.

When to Get Help   How can parents tell when they need such professional help from a psychologist or psychiatrist? "Parents need to look at their child's functioning in the important spheres in a child's life," explains Dr. Nathanson. "His or her attendance in school, for one. And once in school, does he concentrate and perform the work adequately?

"Does your child have significant attachments to peers? And do they look like solid relationships? Are the children basically of the same general age? Is your child well integrated into the group? And does he or she have a best friend?

To be optimally functional, children need solid peer relationships. Peer relationships represent extra-familial attachments, and these are very important developmentally for children."

Another important sphere is home life, continues Dr. Nathanson. "How are your child's relationships with his or her siblings? With each parent? And with the parents as a unit? Does your child have rights and responsibilities commensurate with his age and position in the family? Does he, for instance, have chores? Maybe he can't vacuum anymore because dust triggers his asthma, but does he wash the dishes? Does she have a later bedtime than her younger sib, even though she has asthma? It is really important that parents have a sense of where the child should be, developmentally, at a given point in time." What is appropriate for a five-year-old child is not appropriate for a ten-year-old or a fifteen-year-old.

"And you certainly should look at your child's medical status. Sometimes, your physician will be saying, 'This isn't jibing. Your child is having too many attacks. It doesn't make sense medically.' "

Dysfunctional Family Patterns When a child is first diagnosed with asthma, "there is a certain period of time when it is appropriate for the family to get organized around the disease." However, you should be aware, warns Dr. Nathanson, "that this can sometimes solidify into dysfunction," that is, into family patterns of interacting that may not work well, that may not best serve the needs and interests of either your asthmatic child or the other members of your family.

Such family patterns do not *cause* asthma, of course. As we have seen throughout this book, asthma is a very real physiological disease. The National Heart, Lung and Blood Institute's 1991 Expert Panel Report on asthma emphasizes that "asthma is not caused by psychological factors."

However, some family patterns may contribute to a child's suffering more asthma attacks, missing more days of school and being hospitalized more frequently than the doctors believe is warranted by the child's medical condition. "There can be a psychosomatic flavor to a child's having asthma attacks," says Dr. Nathanson.

To have asthma, a child must first have the genetic endowment and be exposed to the triggers, says Alberto C. Serrano, M.D., Psychiatrist-in-Chief and Director of the Psychiatry Division at The Children's Hospital of Philadelphia and Medical Director of the Philadelphia Child Guidance Clinic. However, then "there are certain family configurations, certain kinds of parenting that can inadvertently reinforce that and may keep a child wheezing."

In extreme cases, "the seriousness of the condition can be exaggerated to the point where the child could become a psychological cripple," Dr. Serrano continues, "and the psychological handicap appears more serious than the physical handicap. The child and the family may act as if the child indeed is more handicapped than he is medically." Again, this situation is not unique to asthma; it can also occur with diabetes and other chronic diseases.

OVERPROTECTIVE PARENTS One common family pattern is that "parents become overprotective—or one parent becomes overprotective—of the child," says Dr. Nathanson. "The diagnosis can provoke so much anxiety that the parents become smothering and all-engulfing."

"A child who has asthma, who obviously feels very helpless and dependent," adds Dr. Serrano, "often tends to have parents who are very doting, very loving, very dedicated and very worried. There is a sense of overinvolvement. It is important, in some cases, for a family to learn when and how to use a certain dose of benign neglect."

One parent's overprotectiveness of an asthmatic child may make the other parent—and other siblings—feel excluded. It also can keep the child with asthma from developing the independence that he needs and from learning how to take care of his asthma himself: how to take his medications, how to recognize and avoid the circumstances that trigger his attacks, how to sense the early warning signs of attacks. "Too much involvement," emphasizes Dr. Serrano, "could lead to excessive dependency in an asthmatic child."

By the time a child with asthma reaches school age, says Dr. Nathanson, he or she should be developing some sense of autonomy, and "it is very important that a parent be helping him to become increasingly in control of his own care." Patrick's mother, for instance, has made it a point to make sure that Patrick—who, at age seven, is in the first grade—knows how to use his inhaler and spacer on his own, so that she does not have to worry about him as much. "If Patrick did get into trouble at school," she explains, "he could take care of it himself."

On the other hand, Douglas, at the age of twelve, remains remarkably uninformed about his asthma and the medications that he is supposed to be taking, even though he has had very severe asthma since he was two years old. "Douglas is certainly old enough to take his own medicines, yet he takes them skittishly," says Dr. Nathanson, "and he stays out of school a *lot*."

Douglas also has an extremely overprotective mother, explains Dr. Nathanson. Mrs. K. talks for the boy and also often helps him put on his clothes. "And she is always terrified that he is going to die." On the days that Douglas does go to school, Mrs. K. "literally sits by her phone in case the school calls. She *cannot* get out." Douglas's physicians believe that she probably keeps him home from school unnecessarily, that she too often thinks he is too sick to go out when he is actually quite well enough.

"It isn't just that Douglas can't understand his asthma management intellectually. It is partly because that would challenge the system. Were he to become more knowledgeable, he would be different in that system and it would change things. Among the complicating factors is the fact that his mother is really going to be 'unemployed' if Douglas becomes more competent at controlling his symptoms.

"This is not an uncommon scenario, the scenario of the unemployed one. Douglas's asthma became an excellent focus for it. The asthma is something around which to organize —organize her anxiety, organize her life." In such families, "a tremendous amount of the parenting function can get stuck around a child's asthma or other chronic disease."

BLAMING ALLERGIES FOR OTHER PROBLEMS In another classic pattern, a family may try to blame allergies and asthma for problems that actually have other roots. Two-year-old Rosalind has allergic rhinitis and asthma that are "basically controlled by medication," says Dr. Nathanson. "They are not life-threatening nor causing her pain." She also has very disruptive behavior. "Her behavior is seriously disturbed. She has major temper tantrums and does dangerous things. The problem is the girl's behavior. Her family needs therapy; her allergies and asthma are not causing her behavior."

Rosalind's mother, however, is "obsessed that there are more allergies. She has read all the books and has seen the best doctors and is still searching. She is looking for the locus of Rosalind's behavior to be in her allergies, in her nose. She is saying, 'My child is acting like this because she is allergic to yet something else that you doctors have not yet discovered.'

"There are many families like this, families that say, 'We know there is something more wrong, something that the doctors haven't yet found that will make this problem instantly controllable.'"

A WAY OF GETTING ATTENTION In another common pattern, asthma or other chronic disease may function as a way that a child can get more attention in a family. Nine-year-old Kenny does not take his medicine regularly, constantly fights with his mother about taking it and has more asthma attacks and is hospitalized more than makes sense medically. Kenny is also a difficult boy in other ways. Although he is bright, he behaves so badly in school that he has been kicked out of several.

One factor in Kenny's life is that he has an older brother, Bill, a high school junior, who is "the golden boy of the family. Bill is really successful, a good student," says Dr. Nathanson. "He does really well academically." And Mrs. S. is a single mother, raising this family alone, without any help from a spouse or relatives. She is the sole support of the family and must work long hours at a hard job. "This woman does indeed have her hands full. This family is an overtaxed system. And Mrs. S. is favoring Bill over Kenny. Bill is easier to favor.

"The dynamic in the family, though, is that Kenny's identity in this family is bound up with his asthma. That is his handle in the family. It has been the way that he can get nurturance and affection. The older brother is The Star, and Kenny is The Sick Kid, The Bad Boy. The only way that Mrs. S. can recognize Kenny, cuddle him figuratively, is when he is sick. Otherwise he just gets ignored.

"It is a family where Kenny doesn't have many other possibilities. It is only in the asthmatic-child role where he is nurtured. He needs to take his medication more reliably, which he should be able to do himself. This child should be more autonomous than he is. For Kenny, conceivably, if he had gone along with that, he wouldn't have had any room for obtaining warmth and nurturing. He and his mother really need to figure out ways to be with each other that are positive and fun for both of them and that don't revolve around his asthma."

This is not something that Kenny thought out consciously, stresses Dr. Nathanson. "I am not suggesting at all that this is a willful process, that a child says, 'I am going to have an asthma attack' to get attention." Also, there is not just one factor responsible for these family patterns of interactions. "These things are always multiply determined."

AVOIDING OTHER CONFLICTS Arguments over a child's taking his or her asthma medications can sometimes be a family's way of avoiding conflicts over other issues. Eleven-year-old Monica, who has severe allergic asthma, takes her medications, but it is always a struggle, and she has been hospitalized many times.

The real issue in this family is conflict between Mrs. G., Monica's mother, and *her* mother, Monica's grandmother, who helps take care of Monica. Monica "is caught, triangulated in this system," says Dr. Nathanson. "It isn't clear in some ways who is in charge, to whom she is the daughter, on whom she is supposed to rely. And why can't the mom and grandmother settle their differences? This family can't talk about these issues, so the conflict has become seated around Monica's medication."

EFFECTS OF EMOTIONS While emotional stress does not cause allergies and asthma, a child's emotions clearly can exacerbate them. Dorothy suspects that one of the reasons her eczema flared up so badly when she was in seventh and eighth grade may have been the emotional stress of going to a new school for junior high. And for some children who have asthma, emotions can be one of the many factors that can trigger acute attacks. Kenny, for one, tends to start wheezing whenever he and his mother get into a yelling match.

More commonly, "a child's feelings can affect the course of the disease," Dr. Nathanson explains. "It is not often clear-cut that a child gets angry and then has an attack. More often, a child has an asthma attack for whatever reason, and then his or her emotions come into play. They may escalate the attack and make it worse, or they may interfere with the child's handling of the attack. Severe anger or anxiety or frustration can affect how well the child copes with the attack, and he or she is not as well able to head it off at the pass."

A child may sometimes use his or her asthma to head off family arguments. "A child can sometimes feel responsible for protecting the family. When there is a high level of tension, Dad is getting angry with Mom and Mom is getting anxious and starts to weep, that's when children often act up and distract. Suddenly everybody's looking at the child. In a family where there is a chronic illness like asthma, a child may begin to have symptoms at those times."

Again, this is not something the child thinks out consciously, Dr. Nathanson stresses, "but the tension may be an emotional trigger, and the child's symptoms can function very effectively as a detouring mechanism. As the tension escalates, the child starts having an asthma attack. The father's criticism of the mother is forgotten. Mom doesn't start to cry. They focus on the child, and there is an air of togetherness. This can reinforce a child's asthma symptoms in a major way."

A FOCUS FOR OTHER CONCERNS Sometimes a child's asthma may become a focus for other family concerns. Thirteen-year-old Geraldine has severe allergies and asthma, and her parents are worried that she never wants to go out at all, that she just wants to stay home with them.

Geraldine's story is that she does sometimes want to go out with her friends and that her father will not let her. Her father has conflicting feelings. "At first, he was very vocal about being disturbed that she never wants to go out," says Dr. Nathanson. "But then he said, 'It's a dangerous world out there. I'm afraid she'll stop breathing. I'm afraid she'll have problems.'

"In fact, Geraldine is a girl who is really not being allowed to progress developmentally. Mrs. K. is also worried about Geraldine but is better able to see her as a girl with developing needs and that they will have to take some chances. There is, in fact, conflict between the mother and father about how to let this girl be launched into adolescence. The father is terribly frightened. And Geraldine responds by often not asking to go out.

"When Geraldine does ask to go out, her parents often disagree about how to handle her request. Then they argue, which pitches the girl into more anxiety. Her parents' arguing is very, very frightening for Geraldine. The meaning of her staying in has become clear. Her staying close to home maintains a homeostasis in this family, but at a cost to Geraldine of her growth and mastery and sense of independence.

"It is not that Geraldine might have an asthma attack that is the real worry. The true issues are: how do you deal with a child's growing up, with issues of, for example, adolescent sexuality? How do you deal with pressures that may come from peers about drugs or alcohol? This family shows how concern over asthma can be a red herring."

As we mentioned at the beginning of this chapter, only a very small proportion of all allergic and asthmatic children and their families ever have any of these problems significantly enough that they need professional assistance from psychologists or psychiatrists.

"It's important for parents to know that for the most part children and families can cope with having allergies and asthma just fine," Dr. Nathanson emphasizes. "Most of them can incorporate the diagnosis and then move on to the rest of their lives."

Index